Defoe
Abbott
Marx
Hardy
Melville
Montaigne
Machiavelli
Haggard
Chesterton
Cooper
Emerson
Joyce
Austen
Hugo
Eliot
Grimm
Stoker
Carroll
Christie
Maupassant
Byron
Molière
Schiller
Wilde
Garnett
Einstein
Fitzgerald
Engels
Smith
Kafka
Goethe
Hawthorne
Hall
Cotton
Dostoyevsky
Willis
Baum
Henry
Kipling
Doyle
Leslie
Dumas
Flaubert
Turgenev
Nietzsche
Balzac
Stockton
Vatsyayana
Crane
Burroughs
Verne
Curtis
Tocqueville
Vinci
Homer
Widger
Tolstoy
Whitman
Gogol
Busch
Darwin
Thoreau
Twain
Potter
Zola
Scott
Plato
Harte
Kant
Freud
Jowett
Stevenson
Dickens
Burton
Hesse
London
Descartes
Cervantes
Andersen
Poe
Aristotle
Wells
Voltaire
Cooke
Hale
James
Hastings
Bunner
Shakespeare
Irving
Richter
Chambers
da
Doré
Dante
Chekhov
Shaw
Wodehouse
Benedict
Alcott
Swift
Pushkin
Newton

 tredition®

tredition was established in 2006 by Sandra Latusseck and Soenke Schulz. Based in Hamburg, Germany, tredition offers publishing solutions to authors and publishing houses, combined with world-wide distribution of printed and digital book content. tredition is uniquely positioned to enable authors and publishing houses to create books on their own terms and without conventional manu-facturing risks.

For more information please visit: www.tredition.com

TREDITION CLASSICS

This book is part of the TREDITION CLASSICS series. The creators of this series are united by passion for literature and driven by the intention of making all public domain books available in printed format again - worldwide. Most TREDITION CLASSICS titles have been out of print and off the bookstore shelves for decades. At tredi-tion we believe that a great book never goes out of style and that its value is eternal. Several mostly non-profit literature projects pro-vide content to tredition. To support their good work, tredition donates a portion of the proceeds from each sold copy. As a reader of a TREDITION CLASSICS book, you support our mission to save many of the amazing works of world literature from oblivion. See all available books at www.tredition.com.

Project Gutenberg

The content for this book has been graciously provided by Project Gutenberg. Project Gutenberg is a non-profit organization founded by Michael Hart in 1971 at the University of Illinois. The mission of Project Gutenberg is simple: To encourage the creation and distribu-tion of eBooks. Project Gutenberg is the first and largest collection of public domain eBooks.

The Development of Embroidery in America

Candace Wheeler

Imprint

This book is part of TREDITION CLASSICS

Author: Candace Wheeler
Cover design: Buchgut, Berlin – Germany

Publisher: tredition GmbH, Hamburg - Germany
ISBN: 978-3-8472-3974-1

www.tredition.com
www.tredition.de

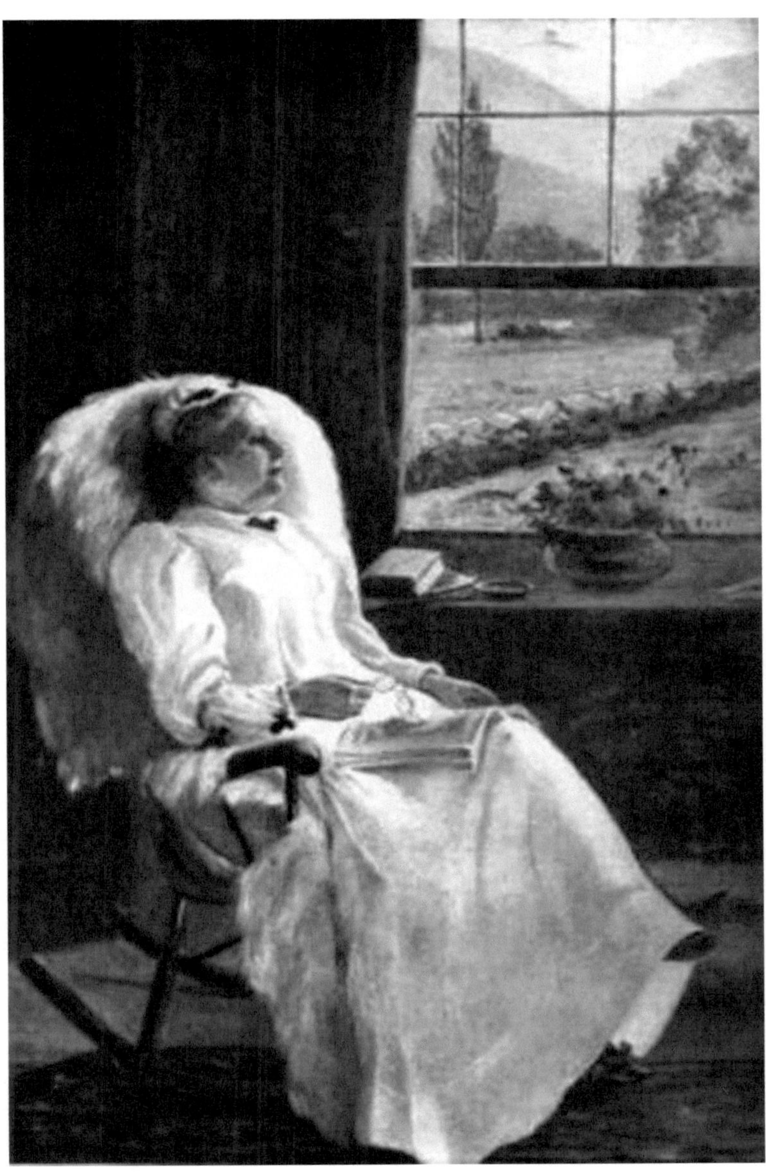

Painted by Dora Wheeler Keith

CANDACE WHEELER
From the painting by her daughter Dora Wheeler Keith.

THE DEVELOPMENT OF EMBROIDERY IN AMERICA

By
CANDACE WHEELER

Illustrated

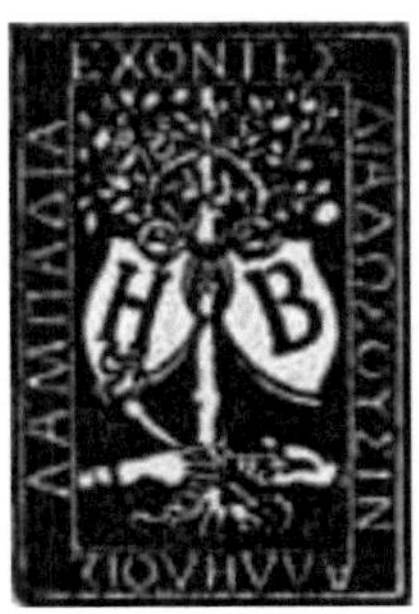

CONTENTS

ILLUSTRATIONS [vii]

THE DEVELOPMENT OF EMBROIDERY IN AMERICA

INTRODUCTORY THE STORY OF THE NEEDLE

The story of embroidery includes in its history all the work of the needle since Eve sewed fig leaves together in the Garden of Eden. We are the inheritors of the knowledge and skill of all the daughters of Eve in all that concerns its use since the beginning of time.

When this small implement came open-eyed into the world it brought with it possibilities of well-being and comfort for races and ages to come. It has been an instrument of beneficence as long ago as "Dorcas sewed garments and gave them to the poor," and has been a creator of beauty since Sisera gave to his mother "a prey of needlework, 'alike on both sides.'" This little descriptive phrase—alike on both sides—will at once suggest to all needlewomen a perfection of method almost without parallel. Of course it can be done, but the skill of it must have been rare, even in those far-off days of leisure when duties and pleasures did not crowd out painstaking tasks, and every art was carried as far as human assiduity and invention could carry it. [4]

A history of the needlework of the world would be a history of the domestic accomplishment of the world, that inner story of the existence of man which bears the relation to him of sunlight to the plant. We can deduce from these needle records much of the physical circumstances of woman's long pilgrimage down the ages, of her mental processes, of her growth in thought. We can judge from the character of her art whether she was at peace with herself and the world, and from its status we become aware of its relative importance to the conditions of her life.

There are few written records of its practice and growth, for an art which does not affect the commercial gain of a land or country is not apt to have a written or statistical history, but, fortunately in this case, the curious and valuable specimens which are left to us tell their own story. They reveal the cultivation and amelioration of domestic life. Their contribution to the refinements are their very existence.

A history of any domestic practice which has grown into a habit marks the degree of general civilization, but the practice of needle-work does more. To a careful student each small difference [5] in the art tells its own story in its own language. The hammered gold of Eastern embroidery tells not only of the riches of available material, but of the habit of personal preparation, instead of the mechanical. The little Bible description of captured "needlework alike on both sides" speaks unmistakably of the method of their stitchery, a cross-stitch of colored threads, which is even now the only method of stitch "alike on both sides."

It is an endless and fascinating story of the leisure of women in all ages and circumstances, written in her own handwriting of pains-taking needlework and an estimate of an art to which gold, silver, and precious stones—the treasures of the world—were devoted. More than this, its intimate association with the growth and well-being of family life makes visible the point where savagery is left behind and the decrees of civilization begin.

I knew a dear Bible-nourished lonely little maid who had constructed for herself a drama of Eve in Eden, playing it for the solitary audience of self in a corner of the garden. She had brought all manner of fruits and had tied them to the fence palings under the apple boughs. This little Eve [6] gathered grape leaves and sewed them carefully into an apron, the needle holes pierced with a thorn and held together by fiber stripped from long-stemmed plantain leaves. Here she and her audience of self hid under the apple boughs and waited for the call of the Lord.

The long ministry of the needle to the wants of mankind proves it to have been among the first of man's inventions. When Eve sewed fig leaves she probably improvised some implement for the process, and every daughter of Eve, from Eden to the present time, has been indebted to that little implement for expression of herself in love and duty and art. For this we must thank the man who, the Bible relates, was "the father of all such as worked in metals, and made needles and gave them to his household." He is the first "handy man" mentioned in history — blest be his memory!

If the day should ever come, not, let us hope, in our time or that of our children, when the manufacturer shall find that it no longer pays to make needles, what value will attach to individual specimens! If they were only to be found in occasional bric-à-brac shops or in the collections of some far-seeing hoarder of rarities, it would be [7] difficult to overrate the interest which might attach to them. How, from the prodigal disregard of ages and the mysteries of the past, would emerge, one after another, recovered specimens, to be examined and judged and classified and arranged!

Perhaps collections of them will be found in future museums under different headings, such as:

"Needles of Consolation," under which might come those which Mary Stuart and her maids wrought their dismal hours into pathetic bits of embroidery during the long days of captivity, or the daughter of the sorrowful Marie Antoinette mended the dilapidations of the pitiful and ragged Dauphin; or:

"Needles of Devotion," wielded by canonized and uncanonized saints in and out of nunneries; or:

"Needles of History," like those with which Matilda stitched the prowess of William the Conqueror into breadths of woven flax.

Possibly there may arise needle experts who, upon microscopic examination and scientific test, will refer all specimens to positive date and peculiar function, and by so doing let in floods of light upon ancient customs and habits. It is idle [8] to speculate upon a condition which does not yet exist, for, happily, needles for actual hand sewing are yet in sufficient demand to allow us to indulge in their purchase quite ungrudgingly.

I was once shown a needle — it was in Constantinople — which the dark-skinned owner declared had been treasured for three hundred years in his family, and he affirmed it so positively and circumstantially that I accepted the statement as truth. In fact, what did it matter? It was an interesting lie or an interesting truth, whichever one might consider it, and the needle looked quite capable of sustaining another century or so of family use. Its eye was a polished triangular hole made to carry strips of beaten metal, exactly such as we read of in the Bible as beaten and cut into strips for embroidery upon linen, such embroidery, in fact, as has often been burned in order to sift the pure gold from its ashes.

Not only the history, but the poetry and song of all periods are starred with real and ideal embroideries—noble and beautiful ladies, whose chief occupations seem to have been the medicining of wounds received in their honor or defense, or the broidering of scarfs and sleeves with which to [9] bind the helmets of their knights as they went forth to tourney or to battle. In these old chronicles the knights fought or made music with harp or voice, and the women ministered or made embroidery, and so pictured lives which were lived in the days of knights and ladies drifted on. The sword and the needle expressed the duties, the spirit, and the essence of their several lives. The men were militant, the women domestic, and wherever in castle or house or nunnery the lives of women were made safe by the use of the sword the needle was devoting itself to comforts of clothing for the poor and dependent, or luxuries of adornment for the rich and powerful. So the needle lived on through all the civilizations of the old world, in the various forms which they developed, until it was finally inherited by pilgrims to a new world, and was brought with them to the wilderness of America.

CHAPTER I   BEGINNINGS IN THE NEW WORLD [10]

The history of embroidery in America would naturally begin with the advent of the Pilgrim Mothers, if one ignored the work of native Indians. This, however, would be unfair to a primitive art, which accomplished, with perfect appropriateness to use and remarkable adaptation of circumstance and material, the ornamentation of personal apparel.

The porcupine quill embroidery of American Indian women is unique among the productions of primitive peoples, and some of the dresses, deerskin shirts, and moccasins with borders and flying designs in black, red, blue, and shining white quills, and edged with fringes hung with the teeth and claws of game, or with beautiful small shells, are as truly objects of art as are many things of the same decorative intent produced under the best conditions of civilization.

To create beauty with the very limited resources of skins, hair, teeth, and quills of animals, colored with the expressed juice of plants, was a problem very successfully solved by these dwellers [11] in the wilderness, and the results were practically and æsthetically valuable.

In the Smithsonian Institution at Washington, D. C., there has happily been preserved a most interesting collection of these early efforts. The small deerskin shirts worn as outer garments by the little Sioux were perhaps among the most interesting and elaborate. They are generally embroidered with dyed moose hair and split quills of birds in their natural colors, large split quills or flattened smaller quills used whole. The work has an embossed effect which is very striking. A coat for an adult of Sioux workmanship, made of calfskin thicker and less pliant than the deerskin ordinarily used for garments, carries a broad band of quill embroidery, broken by whorls of the same, the center of each holding a highly decorated tassel made of narrow strips of deerskin, bound at intervals with split porcupine quills. These ornamental tassels carry the idea of decoration below the bands, and have a changeable and living effect which is admirable. In a smaller shirt, the whole body is covered at irregular intervals with whorls of the finest porcupine quill work, edged by a border of interlaced [12] black and white quills, finished with perforated shells. Many of the designs are edged with narrow zigzag borders of the split quills in natural colors carefully matched and lapped in very exact fashion. There is one small shirt, made with a decorative border of tanned ermine skins in alternate squares of fur and beautifully colored quill embroidery, not one tint of which is out of harmony with the soft yellow of the deerskin body. The edge of the shirt is finished in very civilized fashion, with ermine tails, each pendant, banded with blue quills, at alternating heights, making a shining zigzag of blue along the fringe. The simplicity of treatment and purity of color in this little garment were fascinating, and must have invested the small savage who wore it with the dignity of a prince.

The mother who evolved the scheme and manner of decoration carried her bit of genius in an uncivilized squaw body, but had none the less a true feeling for beauty, and in this mother task lifted the plane of the art of her people to a higher level.

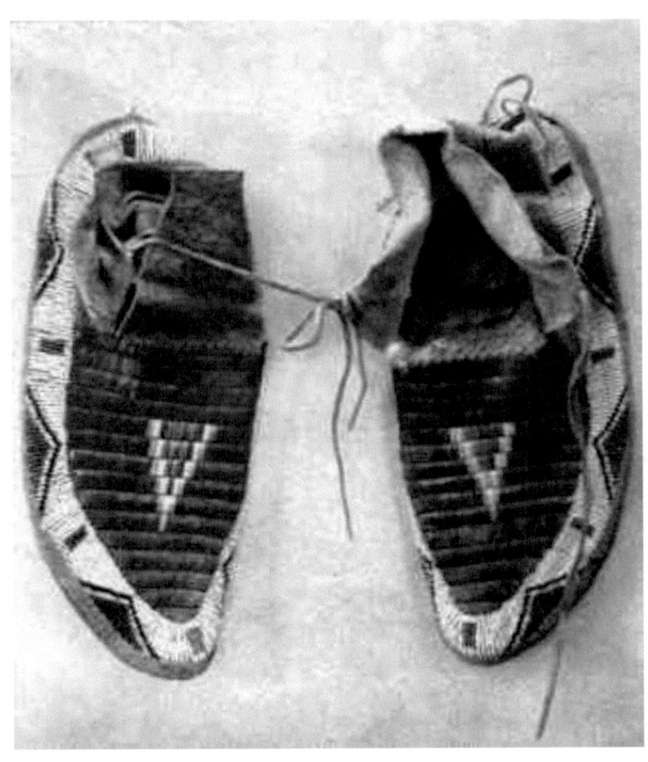

larger image

MOCCASINS of porcupine quillwork, made by Sioux Indians.

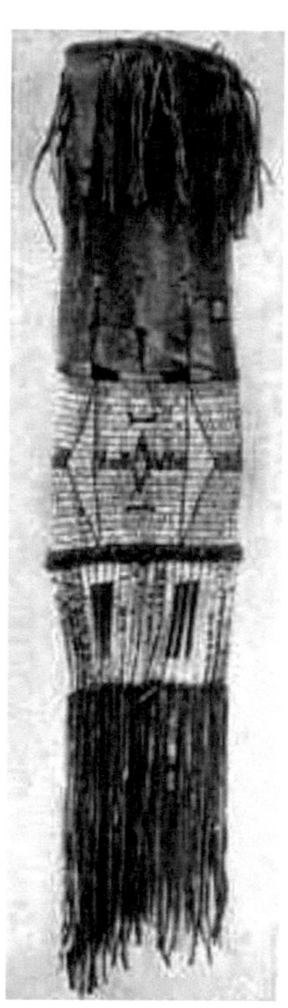

larger image

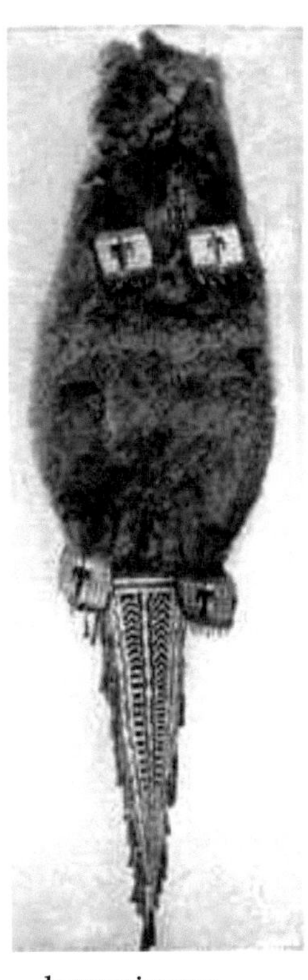

larger image

Courtesy of American Museum of Natural History, New York

PIPE BAGS of porcupine quillwork, made by Sioux Indians.

The purely decorative ability which lived and flourished before the advent of civilization lost its distinctive simplicity of character when woven [13] cloth of brilliant red flannel and the tempting glamour of colored glass beads came into their horizon, although they accepted these new materials with avidity. Porcupine quill work seems to have been _no_ longer practiced, although a few head-bands of ceremony are to be found among the tribes, and now and then one comes across a veritable treasure, an evidence of long and unremitting toil, which has been preserved with veneration.

Of course many valuable results of the best early embroideries still exist among the Indians themselves.

A very striking feature of both early and late work is the fringing, which plays an important part in the decoration of garments. The fringe materials were generally of the longest procurable dried moose hair, the finely cut strips of deerskin, or, in some instances, the tough stems of river and swamp grasses twisted, braided and interwoven in every conceivable manner, and varied along the depth of the fringes by small perforated shells, teeth of animals, seeds of pine, or other shapely and hard substances which gave variety and added weight. Beads of bone and shell are not uncommon, or small bits of hammered [14] metal. In one or two instances I have seen long deerskin fringes with stained or painted designs, emphasized with seeds or shells at centers of circles, or corners of zigzags. This ingenious use of a decorative fringe gave an effect of elaborate ornament with comparatively small labor.

Perhaps the best lesson we have to learn from this bygone phase of decorative effort is in the possibilities of genuine art, where scant materials of effect are available.

A thoughtful and exact study of early Indian art gives abundant indication of the effect of intimacy with the moods and phenomena of Nature, incident to the lives of an outdoor people.

Many of the designs which decorate the larger pieces, like shirts and blankets, were evidently so inspired. The designs of lengthened and unequal zigzags are lightning flashes translated into embroidery; the lateral lines of broken direction are water waves moving in masses. There are clouds and stars and moons to be found among them, and if we could interpret them we might even find records of the sensations with which they were regarded.

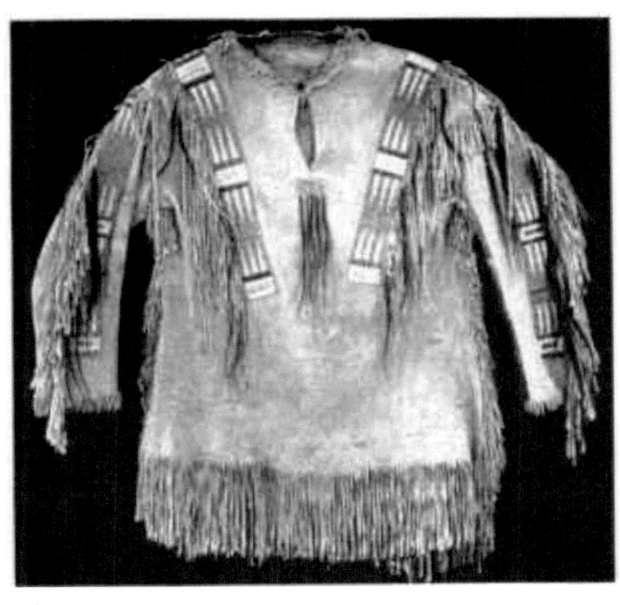

larger image

Courtesy American Museum of Natural History, New York

MAN'S JACKET OF PORCUPINE QUILLWORK
Made by Sioux Indians.

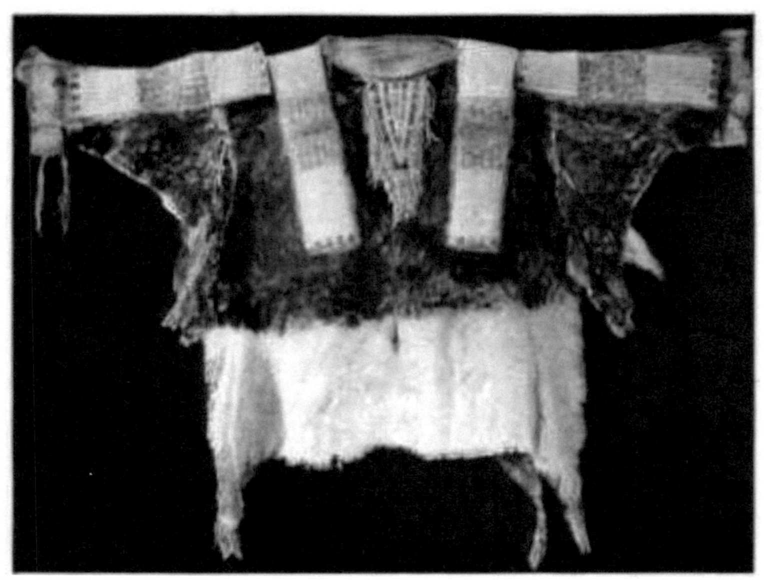

larger image

Courtesy American Museum of Natural History, New York

MAN'S JACKET OF PORCUPINE QUILLWORK
Made by Plains Indians.

It would seem to argue a want of inventive [15] faculty, that the aboriginal women never conceived the idea of weaving fibers together in textiles, but were contented with the skins of animals for warmth of body covering. The two alternatives of so close and warm a substance as tanned skins, or nakedness, seem to a civilized mind to demand some intermediate substance. This, however, was not felt as a want, at least not to the extent of inspiring a textile. Perhaps we should never have had the unique porcupine quill embroidery except for the close-grained skin foundation, which made it possible and permanent. Certainly the cleverness with which the idea of weaving has been used in the evolution of the Indian blanket shows that only the initial thought was lacking. The subsequent use of the arts of spinning and weaving, with the retention of the original idea of decoration in design and coloring, has made the Indian blanket an article of great commercial value.

Fortunately, these productions are valuable to their producers, and even to other members of the tribes, and were carefully preserved from casualties, so that there are still many examples of Indian manufacture, such as belts of wampum, [16] and headbands of ceremony, to be found among existing tribes.

These early specimens are not only intrinsically valuable, but give many a clue to what may be called the spiritual side of the aborigines. They had not learned the limits of representation, and as this history deals with results of life and not with the impulse toward expression which lies at the root of design, we need not attempt more than a suggestion of some of the results. The unguided impulses of Indian art, as seen or imagined in their work, lies behind the work itself and can be read only by its materialization.

CHAPTER II ✿ THE CREWELWORK OF OUR PURITAN MOTHERS [17]

The crewelwork of New England was the first ornamental stitchery practiced in this country by women of European race, and in their hands made its first appearance even during the days of privation and nights of fear which were their portion in this strange new world to which they had come.

The seed of it was brought by that winged creature of destiny, the *Mayflower*, hidden in the folds or decorating the borders of the precious household linen which was a part of the gear of the first Pilgrims. In its hollow interior there was room for bed dressings and table napery, even when the high-posted bedsteads and tables which they had adorned were abandoned, or exchanged for peace of mind and liberty of action.

It may have declared itself in the very first years of settlement, before they had encountered the savage antagonism of the aborigines, and while they still had only the privations incident [18] to pioneer life; or it may have been after the long struggle for ascendancy and possession was over, and they could settle down in hard-won homes. Upon neighboring or contiguous farms there they gradually drew together the threads of memory concerning former peaceful occupations, and wove them once more into the warp of daily life. They could visit one another, exchanging domestic experiences, or reminiscences of spiritual struggles of their own or of fellow Pilgrims, and old-time hand occupations would be a mutual lullaby and an exorcism of anxiety.

The real beginning of embroidery as a national art was probably at a later period, for its previous practice would be but a continuation of old-world occupations or diversions of life.

The devoted mothers of the American race, who sailed the seas in those far-off days, might have brought some favorite "piece" of embroidery among their most intimate belongings, wherewithal to while away the hours of weary days upon the limitless breadths of ocean. There would be intervals of calm between storms, and periods when even the merest shred of a home-practiced art would be doubly and trebly valued, [19] like a piece of heavenly raiment to a naked and banished angel.

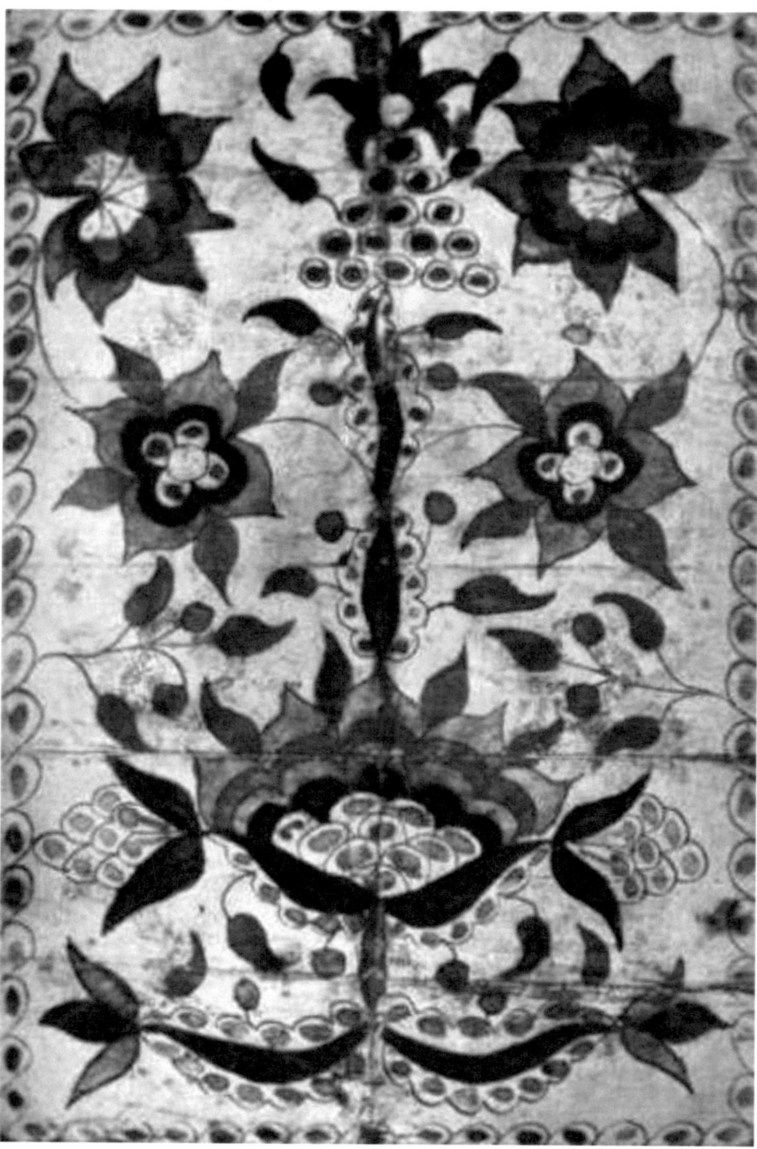

larger image

CREWEL DESIGN, drawn and colored, which dates back to Colonial times.

In the possession of the Dunham family of Cooperstown.

The most natural effort of the woman standing in the midst of such new and strenuous conditions as surrounded the Pilgrim mothers in America, would be to reproduce something which had meant peace and tranquillity in former days. We can imagine her, searching the closely packed iron-bound chests which held most of the worldly goods of the traversing pilgrims—those famous chests, the boards of which had been carefully doweled and faithfully put together to resist outward and inward pressure—packed and re-packed with constant misgivings and hopeful foresight. In those crowded treasure chests it was possible there might be found skeins of crewel, and even working patterns which some hopeful instinct had prompted her to preserve.

While the Puritan mother was scheming to add embroidery to her occupations, she did not forget to train each small maid of the family to the use of the needle. Ruth and Peace and Harmony and Mercy made their samplers as faithfully as though they were growing up under the shade of the apple trees of old England [20] instead of among the blackened stumps of newly cut forests.

So the old art survived its transplantation and rooted itself in spite of storms of terror, and during and after the test of fire and blood, and spread, after the manner of art and knowledge, until it became the joy and comfort of a new race, a vehicle of feminine dexterity and an expression of the creative instinct with which in a greater or lesser degree we are all endowed.

We can easily believe that stores of linen and precious china, as well as the small wheels for the spinning of the flax, could not be denied to the devoted women who chose to share the hard fortunes of their Pilgrim husbands and fathers. It is probable that in one form or another possessions of crewel embroidery were transported with them.

I know of no well-authenticated specimen which came in actual substance in that elastic vessel, but undoubtedly there were such, while many and many existed in the minds and memories of the women of the new colony, to come to life and take on actual form, color and substance when the days of their privations were numbered. If [21] such actual treasured things existed and were preserved through the early days of colonial life, every stitch of them would hold within itself traditions of tranquillity in a world where homes stood, and fields were tilled in safety, because of the vast plains of ocean which lay between them and savage tribes.

In the earliest days of the colonies we could hardly expect more than the necessary practice of the needle, but when we come to the second period, when neighborhoods became towns, and cabins grew into more or less well-equipped farmhouses, Puritan women gladly reverted to the accomplishments of pre-American conditions. The familiar crewelwork of England was the form of needlework which became popular.

In looking for materials with which to recreate this art, they had not at that time far to seek. Wool and flax were farm products, necessities of pioneer life, and their manufacture into cloth was a well-understood domestic art.

Domestic animals had shared the tremendous experiment of transplantation of a fragment of the English race, and had suffered, no doubt, with their masters and owners, the struggles with [22] savages and unaccustomed circumstances, but they had survived and increased "after their kind." Even through the strenuous wars against their very existence by uncivilized man, they lived and increased. Cows "calved," and sheep "lambed," and wool in abundance was to be had.

The enterprising Puritan woman pulled the long-fibered straggling lock of wool, sorted out and rejected from the uniform fleeces, carded it with her little hand cards into yard-long finger-sized rolls, and twisted it upon her large wheel spindle, producing much such thread as an Italian peasant woman spins upon her distaff to-day as she walks upon the shore at Baiæ.

If the pioneer was a natural copyist, she doubled and twisted it, to make it in the exact fashion of the English crewel; if adventurous and independent, she worked it single threaded. This yarn had all the pliant qualities necessary for embroidery, and was in fact uncolored crewel.

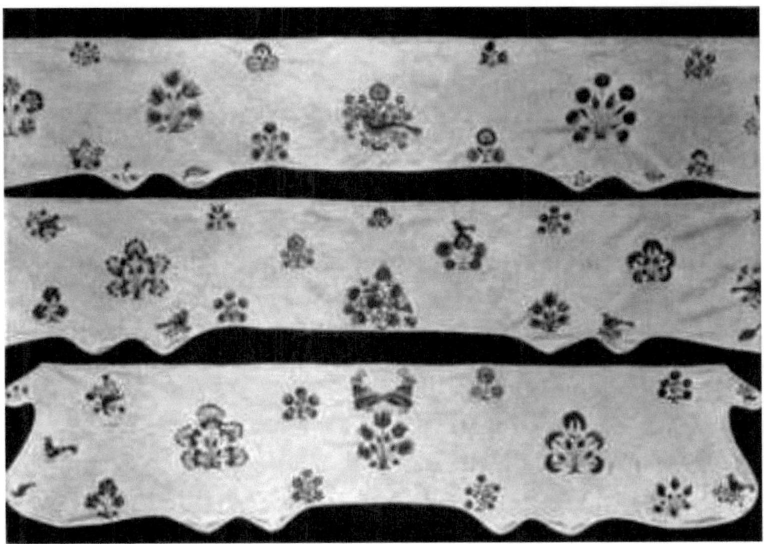

larger image

Courtesy of Essex Institute, Salem, Mass.

TESTER embroidered in crewels in shades of blue on white homespun linen. Said to have been brought to Essex, Mass., in 1640, by Madam Susanna, wife of Sylvester Eveleth.

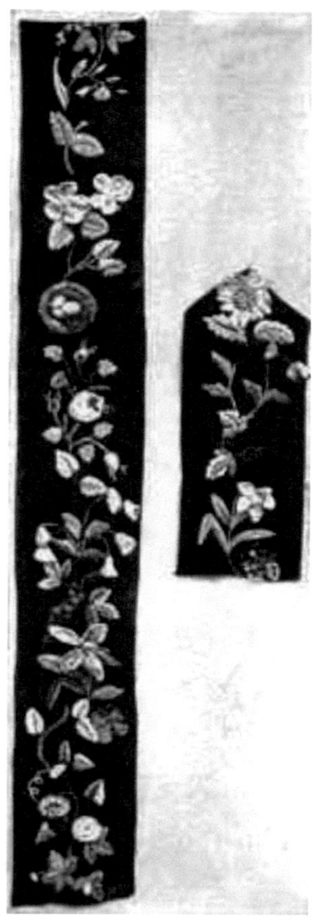

larger image

Raised embroidery on black velvet. Nineteenth century American.

So, also, the production of flax thread, when the crop of flax was grown, and the long stems had struggled upward to their greatest heights, and finished themselves in a cloud of multitudinous [23] blue flax flowers, beautiful enough to be grown for beauty alone, they pulled and made into slender bundles, and laid under the current of the brook which neighbored most pioneer houses, until the thready fibers could be washed and scraped from the vegetable outer coat, the perishable parts of their composition, and combed into separateness. Then it was ready for the small flax wheel of the housewife. Every woman had both wool wheel and flax wheel, the latter of all grades of beauty, from those made for the use of queens and ladies of high degree—royal for elaboration—to the modest ashen wheel, derived from a long line of industrious and careful foremothers, or copied by the clever Pilgrim fathers, from some adventurous wheel which had made the long voyage from civilized Holland to uncivilized America.

For color, the simplest and most at hand expedient was a dip in the universal indigo tub, which waited in every "back shed" of the Puritan homestead. One single dip in its black-looking depths and the skein of spun lamb's wool acquired a tint like the blue of the sky. Immersion of a day and night gave an indelible stain of a darker [24] blue, and a week's repose at the bottom of the pot made the wool as dark in tint as the indigo itself. For variety in her blues, the enterprising housewife used the sunburned "taglocks" which were too hopelessly yellow for webs of white wool weaving, and gave them a short immersion in the tub, with the result of a beautiful blue-green, tinged through and through with a sunny luster, and this color was sun-fast and water-fast, capable of holding its tint for a century.

We know how knots of living wool grow golden by dragging through dew and lying in the sun, and how the ladies of Venice sat upon the roofs of their palaces with locks outspread upon the encircling brims of crownless hats, in order to capture the true Venetian tint of hair. We do not know by what alchemy the sun *silvers* a web spread out to whiten, and yet *gilds* the human tresses of ladies and yellows the "taglocks" of sheep. Chemists may be able to explain, but simple woman, unversed in the mysteries of chemistry, cannot. Whatever may have been the science of it, this golden hue added to medium and dark blue a triad of shades, which proved to be most effective when placed upon pure white [25] of bleached linen, or the gray-cream of the unbleached web.

The color seekers soon learned that every indelible stain was a dye, and if little God-fearing Thomas came home with a stain of ineffaceable green or brown on the knees of his diminutive tow breeches, the mother carefully investigated the character of it, and if it was unmoved by the persuasive influence of "soft soap and sun," she added it to a list which meant knowledge. It is to be hoped that this was often considered an equivalent for the "trouncing" which was the common penalty of accident or inadvertence suffered by the Puritan child. In truth, Solomon's unwholesome caution, "Spare the rod and spoil the child," was all too strictly observed in those conscience-ridden Puritan days. I had a child's lively disapproval of Solomon, since the curse of his sarcastic comment came down with the Puritan strain in my own blood, and I have a smarting recollection of it.

God-fearing Thomas and his brothers added to their mother's artistic equipment not only a list of variously shaded brown from the bark of the black walnut tree, and of yellows from the leaves [26] and twigs of the sumac and wild cherry, but numberless others. She was an untiring color hunter, an experimenter with the juices of plants and flowers and berries, and with every unwash-outable stain. She set herself to the exciting task of repetition and variation. She tried the velvet shell of young butternuts upon threads of her white wool, and found a spring green, and if she spread over it a thinnest wash of hemlock bark, they were olive, and if she dipped them in mitigated indigo, lo! they were of the green of sea hollows. The butternut in all stages of its growth, from the smallest and greenest to the rusty black of the ripe ones, and the blackest black of the dried shell, was a mine of varied color; and the brass kettle of from ten to twenty quarts capacity, which served so many purposes in domestic life, could be tranquilly carrying out some of her propositions in the corner of the wide chimney while dinner was cooking, or in the ashes of the burned-out embers while the household slept.

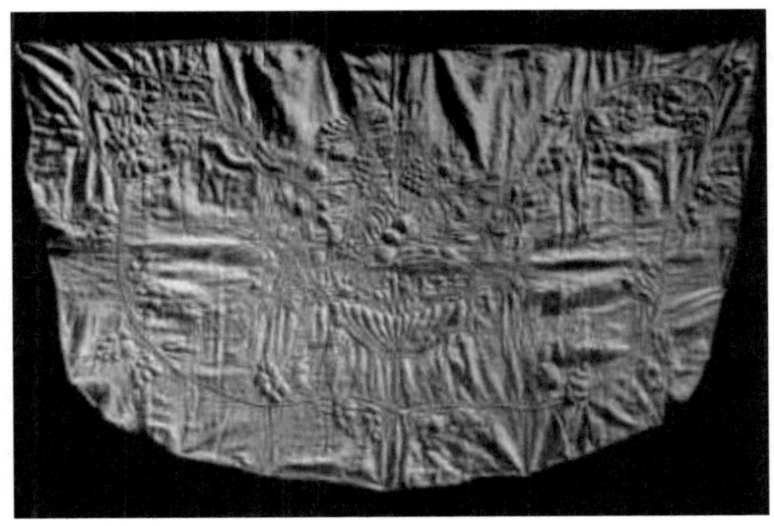

larger image

QUILTED COVERLET made by Ann Gurnee.

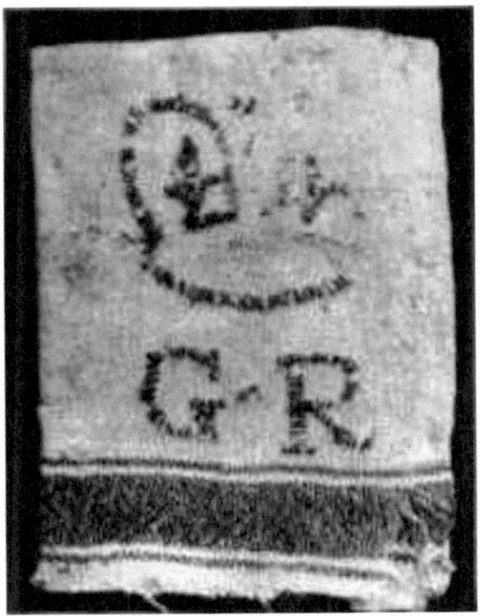

larger image

Courtesy of Bergen County Historical Society, Hackensack, N. J.

HOMESPUN WOOLEN BLANKET with King George's Crown embroidered with home-dyed blue yarn in the corner. From the Burdette home at Fort Lee, N. J., where Washington was entertained.

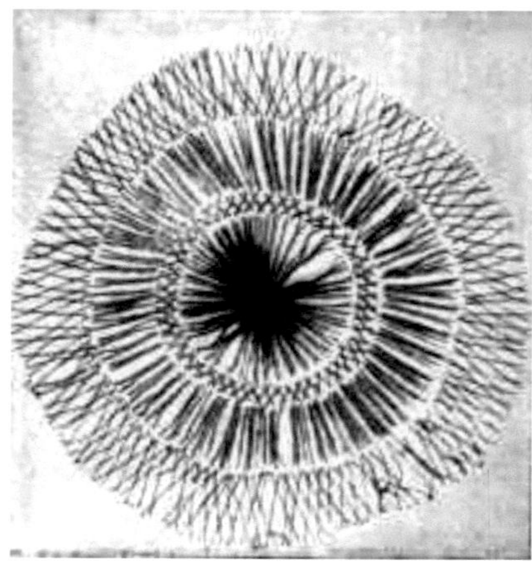

larger image

Courtesy of Bergen County Historical Society, Hackensack, N. J.

CHEROKEE ROSE BLANKET, made about 1830 of homespun wool with "Indian Rose" design about nineteen inches in diameter worked in the corners in home-dyed yarns of black, red, yellow, and dark green. From the Westervelt collection.

It was interesting and skillful work to extract these colors, and the emulation of it and the glory of producing a new one was not without its [27] excitement. There was a certain "fast pink" which was the secret of one ingenious ungenerous Puritan woman, who kept the secret of the dye, when rose pink was the unattainable want of feminine New England. She died without revealing it, and as in those days there were no chemists to boil up her rags and test them for the secret, the "Windham pink," so said my grandmother, "made people sorry for her death, although she did not deserve it." This little neighborly fling passed down two generations before it came to me from the later days of the colony.

Yellows of different complexions were discovered in mayweed, goldenrod and sumac, and the little-girl Faiths and Hopes and

40

Harmonys came in with fingers pink from the handling of pokeberries and purple from blackberry stain, tempting the sight with evanescent dyes which would not keep their color even when stayed with alum and fortified with salt. All this made Mistress Windham's memory the more sad. A good reliable rose red was always wanting. Madder could be purchased, for it was raised in the Southern colonies, but the madder was a brown red. Finally some enterprising merchantman [28] introduced cochineal, and the vacuum was filled. With a judicious addition of logwood, rose red, wine red and deep claret were achieved.

The dye of dyes was indigo, for the blue of heaven, or the paler blue of snow shadows, to a blue which was black or a black which was blue, was within its capacity. And the convenience of it! The indigo tub was everywhere an adjunct to all home manufactures. It dyed the yarn for the universal knitting, and the wool which was a part of the blue-gray homespun for the wear of the men of the household. "One-third of white wool, one-third of indigo-dyed wool, and one-third of black sheep's wool," was the formula for this universal texture. Perhaps it was not too much to say that the gray days of the Pilgrim mother's life were enriched by this royal color.

The soft yarns, carefully spun from selected wool, took kindly to the natural dyes, and our friend, the Puritan housewife, soon found herself in possession of a stock of home-manufactured material, soft and flexible in quality, and quite as good in color as that of the lamented English crewels. The homespun and woven linens with which her chests were stocked were exactly the [29] ground for decorative needlework of the kind which she had known in her English childhood, long before questions of conscience had come to trouble her, or the boy who had grown up to be her husband had been wakened from a comfortable existence by the cat-o'-nine-tails of conscience, and sent across the sea to stifle his doubts in fighting savagery.

Probably the Puritan mother could stop thinking for a while about the training of Thomas and Peace and Harmony, and the rest of the dozen and a half of children which were the allotted portion of every Puritan wife, while she selected out intervals of her long busy days, as one selects out bits of color from bundles of uninteresting patches, and devoted them to absolutely superfluous needlework.

What a joy it must have been to ponder whether she should use deep pink or celestial blue for the flowers of her pattern, instead of remembering how red poor baby Thomas's little cushions of flesh had grown under the smart slaps of her corset board when he overcame his sister Faith in a fair fight about nothing, and what a relief the making of crewel roses must [30] have been from the doubts and cares of a constantly increasing family!

She sorted out her colors, three shades of green, three of cochineal red, two of madder—one of them a real salmon color—numberless shades of indigo, yellows and oranges and browns in goodly bunches, ready for the long stretches of fair solid white linen split into valances or sewed into a counterpane. Truly she was a happy woman, and she would show Mistress Schuyler, with her endless "blue-and-white," what she could do with *her* colors! Then she had a misgiving, and reflected for a moment on the unregeneracy of the human soul, and that poor Mistress Schuyler's quiet airs of superiority really came from her Dutch blood, for her mother was an English Puritan who had married a Hollander, and her own husband revealed to her in the dead of night, when all hearts are opened, his belief that "Brother Schuyler had been moved to emigrate much more by greed of profitable trade with the savages than by longings for liberty of conscience."

She went back to her "pattern," which she just now remembered had been lent her by poor [31] Mistress Schuyler, and was soon absorbed in making long lines of pin pricks along the outlines of the pattern, so that she could sift powdered charcoal through and catch the shapes of leaves and curves on her fair white linen.

Her foot was on the rocker of the cradle all the time, and the last baby was asleep in it. The hooded cherry cradle which had rocked the three girls and four boys, counting the wee velvet-scalped Jonathan, against whose coming the cradle had been polished with rottenstone and whale oil until it shone like mahogany.

Should the roses of the pattern be red or pink? and the columbines blue or purple? She could make a beautiful purple by steeping the sugar paper which wrapped her precious cone of West Indian "loaf sugar," and sugar-paper purple was reasonably fast. So ran the thoughts of the dear, straight-featured Puritan wife as she sorted her colors and worked her pattern.

At this period of her experience of the new life of the colonies, the chief end of her embroidery was to help in creating a civilized home, to add to what had been built simply for shelter and protection, some of the features which lived and [32] grew only in the atmosphere of safety and content. Hospitality was one of the features of New England life, and the first addition to the family shelter was a bedroom, which bore the title of the "best bedroom," and a tall four-post bed, which was the "best bed." The adornment of this holy altar of friendship was an urgent duty.

When I began this allusion to the "best bedroom," I left the housewife sorting her tinted crewels for its adornment, and she still sat, happily cutting the beautiful homespun linen into lengths for the two bed valances, the one to hang from the upper frame which surrounded the top of her four-post bedstead, and the other, which hung from the bed frame itself, and reached the floor, hiding the dark space beneath the bed. The "high-post bedstead" had long groups of smooth flutes in the upward course of its posts, and no footboard, a plain-sawed headboard and smooth headposts. There must be a long curtain at the head of the bed, which would hide both headboard and plain headposts, and this curtain she meant should have a wide border of crewelwork at the top and bunches of flowers scattered at intervals on its surface.

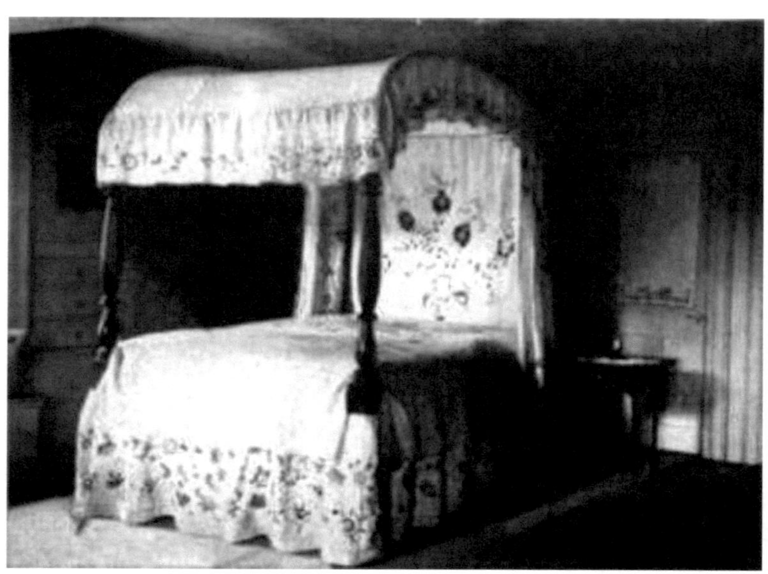

larger image

BED SET. Keturah Baldwin pattern, designed, dyed, and worked by The Deerfield Society of Blue and White Needlework. Deerfield, Mass.

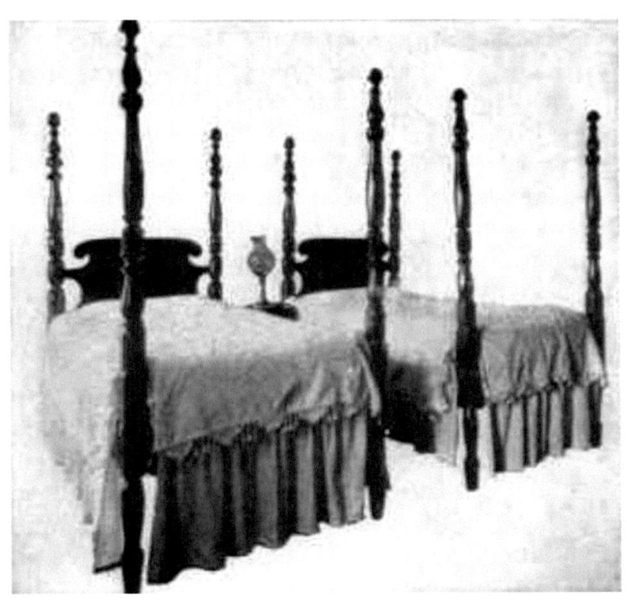

larger image

Courtesy of Colonial Rooms, John Wanamaker, New York

BED COVERS worked in candle wicking.

[33] None of Mistress Schuyler's "blue-and-white" for her! It should carry every color she could muster, and the upper valance should have the same border as the head curtain. The lower valance would not need it, for the counterpane would hang well over, and she meant somehow to bend the border design into a wreath and work it in the center of the counterpane, and double-knot a fringe to go entirely around it, the same as that which should edge the upper valance.

It was a luxurious bed dressing when it was finished, and nothing in it of material to differentiate it from the embroideries which were being done in England at the very time. There were no original features of design or arrangement. The close-lapping stitches were set in exactly the same fashion, and, considering the absolute necessity of growing and manufacturing all the materials, it was a wonderful performance.

It was not alone bed hangings which were subjects of New England crewelwork; there were mantel valances, which covered the plain wooden mantels and hung at a safe distance above the generous household fires. These were wrought with borders of crewelwork, and finished with [34] elaborate thread and crewel fringes. They were knotted into diamond-shaped openings, above the fringes, three or four rows of them, the more the better, for in the general simplicity of furnishing, these things were of value. Then there were table covers and stand covers and wall pockets of various shapes and designs, and, in short, wherever the housewife could legitimately introduce color and ornamentation, crewelwork made its appearance.

In the very infancy of the art of embroidery in America, the primitive needlewoman was possessed of means and materials which fill the embroiderers of our rich later days with envy. Homespun linen is no longer to be had, and dyes are no longer the pure, simple, hold-fast juices which certain plants draw from the ground; and try as we may to emulate or imitate the old embroidered valances which hung from the testers of the high-post bedsteads and concealed the dark cavities beneath, and the coverlet besprinkled with bunches of impossible flowers done in home-concocted shades of color upon heavy snow-white linen, we fall far short of the intrinsic merits of those early hangings. [35]

There are many survivals of these embroideries in New England families, who reverence all that pertains to the lives of their founders. Bed hangings had less daily wear and friction than pertained to other articles of decorative use, and generally maintained a healthy existence until they ceased to be things of custom or fashion. When this time came they were folded away with other treasures of household stuffs, in the reserved linen chest, whence they occasionally emerge to tell tales of earlier days and compare themselves with the mixed specimens of needlework art which have succeeded them, but cannot be properly called their descendants.

The possession of a good piece of old crewelwork, done in this country, is as strong a proof of respectable ancestry as a patent of nobility, since no one in the busy early colonial days had time for such work save those whose abundant leisure was secured by ample means and liberal surroundings. The incessant social and intellectual activity demanded by modern conditions of life was uncalled for. No woman, be she gentle or simple, had stepped from the peaceful obscurity of home into the field of the world to war for its prizes [36] or rewards. If the man to whom she belonged failed to win bread or renown, the women who were bound in his family starved for the one or lived without the luster of the other.

I have shown that even in the early days of flax growing and indigo dyeing the New England farmer's wife had come into her heritage, not only of materials, but of the implements of manufacture. She had the small flax wheel which dwelt in the keeping room, where she could sit and spin like a lady of place and condition, and the large woolen wheel standing in the mote-laden air of the garret, through which she walked up and down as she twisted the yarn.

Later, the colonial dame, if she belonged to the prosperous class—for there were classes, even in the beginning of colonial life—had her beautifully shaped mahogany linen wheel, made by the skillful artificers of England or Holland, more beautiful perhaps, but not more capable than that of the farm wife, whittled and sandpapered into smoothness by her husband or sons, and both were used with the same result.

The pioneer woodworker had a lively appreciation of the new woods of the new country, and [37] made free use of the abundant wild cherry for the furniture called for by the growing prosperity of the settlements, its close grain and warm color giving it the preference over other native woods, excepting always the curly and bird's-eye maple, which were novelties to the imported artisan.

I remember that "curly maple" was a much prized wood in my own childhood, and that after carefully searching for the outward marks of it among the trees of the farm, I asked about the shape of its leaves and the color of its bark, so that I might know it—for children were supposed to know species of trees by sight in my childhood. "Why," said my mother, "it looks like any other maple tree on the outside; it is only that the wood is curly, just as some children have curly hair." Even now, after all these years, a plane of curly maple suggests the curly hair of some child beloved of nature.

The beautiful curly, spotted and satiny maple wood was, however, "out of fashion" when the roving shipmasters began to bring in logs of Santo Domingo mahogany in the holds of their far-wandering barks, and the cabinetmakers to cut beautiful shapes of sideboards, and curving legs [38] and backs of chairs, as well as the tall carved headposts and the head and footboards of luxurious beds from them. It was not only that they were a repetition of English luxury, but that they made more of themselves in plain white interiors, by reason of insistent color, than the blond sisterhood of maples could do. Cherry, which shared in a degree its depth of color, held its world for a longer period, but no wood could withstand the magnificence of pure mahogany red, with the story of its vegetable life written along its planes in lines and waves, deepening into darks, and lightening into ocher and gold along its surfaces.

If the cabinetry of New England is a digression, it is perhaps excusable on the ground of its close connection with the crewel work of New England, of which we are treating, and to which we shall have something of a sense of novelty in returning, since at least the complexion of our colonial embroidery has experienced a change.

So, in spite of the success of the early Puritan woman in producing tints necessary to the various needs of colored crewelwork, the supremacy of indigo as a dye led to a lasting fashion of embroidery [39] known as "blue-and-white." It was the assertion of absolute and tried merit in materials which led to its success. We sometimes see this emergence of persistent goodness in instances of some human career, where indefatigable integrity outruns the glamour of personal gift. This was the fortune of the "blue-and-white," which not only created a style, but has achieved persistence and has broken out in revivals all along the history of American embroidery. It has been somewhat identified with domestic weaving, for the loom has always been a member of the New England family, the great home-built loom, standing in the far end of the kitchen, capable of divers miracles of creation between dawn and sunset.

On this much-to-be-prized background of homespun linen the different shades of indigo blue could be, and were, very effectively used, and it is worthy of note that it repeated the simple contrasts of the Canton china or the "blue Canton" which were the prized gifts brought to their families by the returning New England seamen in the profitable "India trade," which soon became a commercial fact.

"Blue-and-white" had at first been evolved by [40] tight-bound circumstances. Excellent practice in shades of blue had given it a certified place in the embroidery art of America, but we do not find it in collections of old English embroidery. It is one of the small monuments which mark the path of the woman colonist, narrowed by circumstances, which created a recognized style. It is not to be wondered at that blue-and-white crewelwork made a place for itself in the history of embroidery which was a permanent one. The circumstances of Puritan life being so simple and direct would induce a corresponding simplicity of taste, and simplicity is apt to seize upon first principles.

Every colorist knows that strong but peaceful contrast is one of the first laws of color arrangement, and the unconscious yoking of white and blue placed one of the strongest color notes against unprotesting and receptive white. This made a new manner or style of embroidery. Its permanence may have been influenced by the art of one of the oldest peoples of the world, and as we have said, the prevalence of Canton china upon the dressers and filling the mantel closets and serving the tables of the rich, was [41] beginning to appear in all houses of growing prosperity, even where pewter ware and dishes carved from wood still held the place of actual service.

The Puritan housewife could arrange her grades of blue according to the Chinese colors of this oldest domestic art of the world, and be correspondingly happy in the result. Chinese design, however, had no influence in the growing practice of embroidery, and here also an instinctive law prevailed. She recognized that even the highly artificial landscape art of her idolized plates would not suit the flexible and broken surfaces of her equally cherished linen, or the surroundings of her life.

It was small wonder that this became a favorite style of embroidery and has in it the seeds of permanence. A table setting of snow-white or cream-white homespun, scalloped and embroidered in lines of blue crewels, shining with the precious Canton blue, was, and would be even at this day, a thing to admire.

The first deviation from the habitual crewelwork is to be found in the "blue-and-white," for although the same stitch was employed, it [42] was more often in outline than solid. The designs were sketches instead of "patterns" as had formerly been the case. Although this variety of work comes under the head of colonial crewelwork, there was in it the beginning of the changes and variety effected by differing circumstances and influences—those vital circumstances which leave their traces constantly along the history of needlework. It was owing to various reasons that outline embroidery largely took the place of solid crewelwork.

The question of design must have been a rather difficult one, as there were no designs, and almost no sources of design for needlework, and at this stage of the art in New England original design seems not to have suggested itself. It would certainly have been quite natural to have copied pine trees and broken outlines of hills, but as this class of embroidery was almost entirely used for hangings and decorative furnishings, the Pilgrim mothers seem to have had an instinctive sense that such design was incongruous. Consequently they copied English models. We find designs of crewelwork of the period in English museums identically the same as in the New England [43] work, thorned roses and voluminously doubled pinks, held together in borders of long curved lines or scattered at regular intervals in groups and bunches.

My grandmother explained to me in that long-ago period, where her great age and my inquisitive youth met and exchanged our several and individual surplus of thought and talk, that to a certain extent ladies of colonial days copied many of their designs from what were called India chintzes. These chintzes seem to have been the intermediate wear between homespun of either flax or wool and the creamy satins or the thick "paduasoy," the more flexible "lutestring" silks, worn by great ladies of the period, and the wrought India muslins for less conventional occasions. India chintzes were printed upon white or tinted grounds of hand-spun cotton, in colors so generously full of substance as to have almost the effect of brocaded stuffs, and adaptations from their designs were suitable for embroidery. I remember the three-cornered and square bits of India chintz which my grandmother showed me in long-preserved "housewives," or "huz-ifs," as she called them. They [44] were

50

lengths of domestic linen on which small squares or triangles of chintz were sewn, making a series of small pockets, each one stuffed with convenient threads or bits of colored sewing silks, or needle and thimble. These were pinned at the belt of the active housewife, and hung swaying against her skirts if she rose from her sewing, or were conveniently at hand if she sat patching or embroidering. I remember that some of my grandmother's "huz-ifs" still held threads of different colored crewels wound on bits of cardboard, and any embroiderer might envy the convenience of such holders.

I do not see, in fact, why there should not be a revival of "huz-ifs," a pleasant new fashion, founded upon the old, holding in harmonious variety all the wonders of modern manufacture, as well as making mementos of former gowns of one's own and of one's friends. They might be studied gradations of color and design, and be enriched by harmonious bindings. If my dwindling time holds out, perhaps I shall institute or assist at such a renewal of old conveniences, in spite of sharp contrast of purposes, adding to home costume a grace of pendent color. [45]

I was talking of design, when "huz-ifs" intruded, and was saying that at the period when "blue-and-white" took on the "outline practice" design was a difficult question; indeed, it is always a difficult question for embroiderers. It is so important a part or quality of the art of embroidery. In fact, it is the business of the successful embroiderer to know as much about design as she must about stitchery and color.

After the advent of "blue-and-white," embroidery took on many different features. Curiously enough, when it was confined to decorative uses, its character immediately changed. Crewelwork of the period was not given to hangings and furniture, but to clothing. An embroidered apron became of much more importance than a bed valance or counterpane. The young girl began by embroidering her school aprons with borders of forget-me-nots and mullein pinks, in colored crewels.

I remember seeing among my grandmother's savings an apron of gray unbleached linen, quite dark in color, with a border of single pinks entirely around it. The design had evidently been drawn from the flower itself, and the whole [46] performance was essentially different from that of a slightly earlier period. The materials of homespun linen and home-dyed crewels were the same. The thing which was different and showed either a cropping-out of original thought or a bias toward the style of embroidery lately introduced by the famous school of Bethlehem, Pennsylvania, was an over-and-over stitch instead of the old crewel method. This over-and-over stitch was apparent in all crewel embroidery devoted to personal wear, but was never found in articles used for house or decorative purposes. It was certainly a proper distinction, as the *flat* of crewel was not capable of shadow and was more inherently a part of the textile, as much so, indeed, as a stamped or woven decoration would have been.

It was not long before the over-and-over stitch demanded silks and flosses instead of crewels for its exercise, and silk or satin for the background of its exploits. There were satin bags covered with the most delicate stitchery, and black silk aprons with wreaths of myrtle done with silks or flosses, and, finally, satin pelerines exquisitely embroidered in designs of carefully shaded roses. [47] Although nothing remarkable or epoch-making happened in the art of embroidery, it retained an even more than respectable existence. The skill, taste, and love for the creation of beauty, which were the heritage of the race, were kept alive.

CHAPTER III 🌸 SAMPLERS AND A WORD ABOUT QUILTS [48]

A chapter upon Samplers, by right, should precede the discussion of colonial embroidery, although the practice of mothers in crewel-work was simultaneous with it. They were carried on at the same time, but the embroidery was work for grown-up people, while samplers were baby work—a beginning as necessary as being taught to walk or talk, to the future of the child. Fortunately, the very infant interest in samplers has tended to their preservation, and when the child grew to womanhood the sampler became invested with a mingling of family interests and affections, and she, the executant, came to look upon it with motherliness. The loving pride of the mother in the child's accomplishment also tended to the care and preservation of the first work of the small hands.

As late as the twenties of the eighteenth century, infant schools still existed and samplers were wrought by infant fingers. Eighty-five years ago, I myself was in one of a row of little chairs in the infant school, with a small spread of canvas [49] lying over my lap and being sewn to my skirt by misdirected efforts. My box held a tiny thimble and spools of green and red sewing silk, and I tucked it under alternate knees for safety.

Sarah Woodruff!—I wonder where she is now?—sat next to me in my sampler days, and her canvas was white, while mine was yellow. Her border was worked with blue, and mine with green. With a child's inscrutable and wonderful awareness of underlying facts, I knew that Sarah Woodruff's father was richer than mine, and that the white canvas and blue border, which the teacher said "went with it," was an indication of it. I have it now, the little faded yellow parallelogram of canvas, on which the germ of the very fingers with which I am now writing wrought with painstaking care—"Executed by Candace Thurber, her age six years." They have since had various fortunes and experiences, these fingers, and have wrought to the satisfaction, I hope, of their foregone line of Puritan ancestors.

The sampler has special claims upon the world, because it is probable that all forms of textile design originated with it. In fact, design for needlework began with small squares formed [50] by crossing stitches at the junction of textile fiber.

In sequences these squares formed lines, blocks, and corner, and in double-line juxtaposition made the form of border probably the oldest ornamental decoration in the world, generally known as a Roman border. This decoration escaped from textiles into stone and building materials, and in fact appeared in the elaboration of all materials, from the fronts of temples to the ornamentation of a crown. The most ancient examples of design are founded upon a square, and this points inevitably to the stitch covering the crossing of threads, the cross-stitch, which preceded all others and remained the only decorative stitch until weaving sprang into so fine an art that interstices between threads are unnoticeable. Then, and not until then, the long over-stitch, the *opus plumarium*, which we call "Kensington," was invented, and served to make English embroidery famous in early English history. This was the stitch used by the Pilgrim mothers in their crewel embroidery, as we use it to-day in most of our decorative presentations.

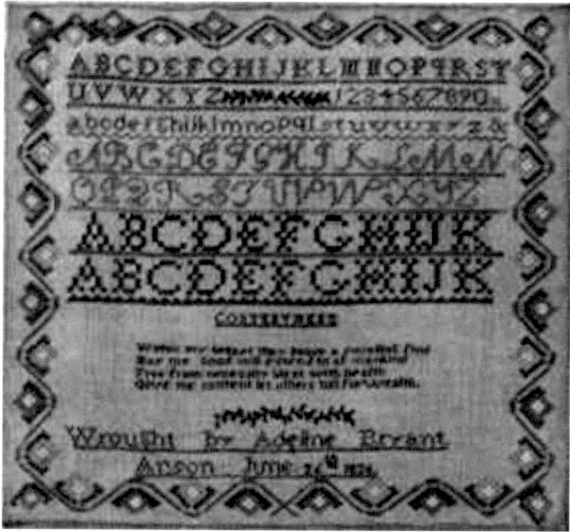

larger image

SAMPLER worked by Adeline Bryant in 1826, now in the possession of Anna D. Trowbridge, Hackensack, N. J.

In spite of the achievements of the *opus plumarium*, [51] we are indebted to simple cross-stitch, to the obligations of the mathematical square of hand weavings, for all the wonderful borderings which have been evolved by ages of the use of the needle, since decoration began. We do not stop to think of the artistic intelligence or gift which made mathematical spaces express beautiful form, any more than we stop in our reading to think of the sensitive intelligence which drew a letter and made it the expression of sound, and yet most of us use the result of some exceptional intelligence and feel the exaltation of what we call culture.

The stitch itself is entitled to the greatest respect, as the very first form of decoration with the needle—an art growing out of and controlled by the earlier art of weaving. Decorative bands of cross-stitch come to us on shreds of linen found in the sepulchers of Egypt and the burial grounds of the prehistoric races of South America. I have seen, in a collection of textiles found in their ancient burial places, the most elaborate and beautiful of cross-stitch borders, wrought into the fabrics which enriched Pizarro's shiploads of loot sent from Vicuna, Peru, to the court of [52] Spain at the time of the wonderful and barbarous "Conquest." All of the old "Roman" borders are found in this collection, the best designs the world has produced, those which architects of the period used upon the fronts and in the interiors of their first creations. And here arises the ever recurring question of thought-sharing between the most widely removed of the earlier human races. How did early Peruvians and far-off Latins think in the same forms, and how did they come to select certain ones as the best, and cleave to them as a common inheritance? But leaving the puzzle of design and returning to the cross-stitch, which was its first interpretation or medium, and to the little Puritans who shared its acquaintance and practice with the women of all ages, we may see how the New England sampler opened the door of inheritance.

As Eve sewed her garments of leaves in the Garden of Eden, so each one of these little Puritan Eves, so far removed in the long history of the race from the first one, was heir to her ingenuities as well as her failings, from her patching together of small and inadequate things, to her creative function in the kingdom of the world, as well as to [53] her attempts to sweeten life, and to her failures and successes.

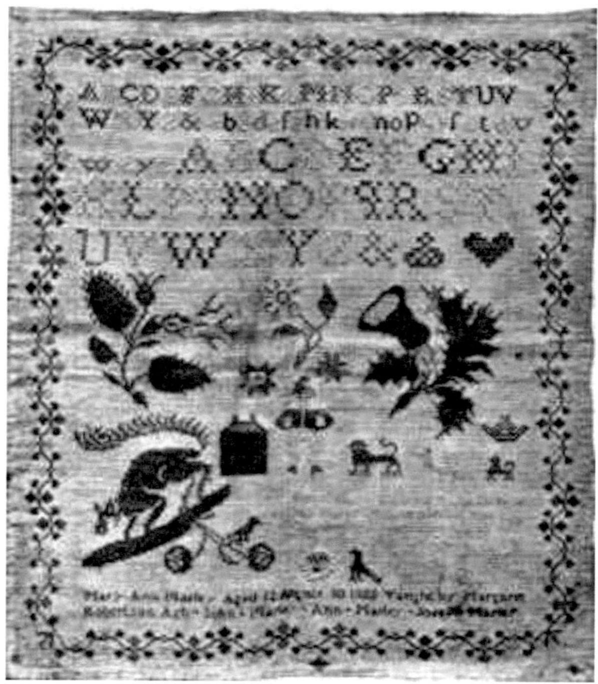

larger image

Courtesy of Essex Institute, Salem, Mass.

SAMPLER embroidered in colors on écru linen, by Mary Ann Marley, aged twelve, August 30, 1820. *From Providence, R. I.*

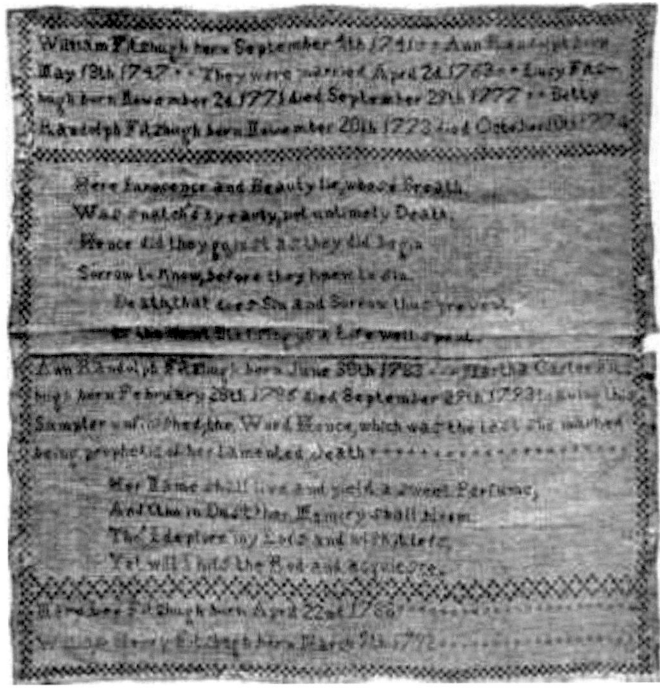

larger image

Courtesy of Essex Institute, Salem, Mass.

SAMPLER embroidered in brown on écru linen, by Martha Carter Fitzhugh, of Virginia, in 1793, and left unfinished at her death.

The learning to do an A or a B in cross-stitch was the beginning of household doing, which is the business of woman's life. The decorative and the useful were evenly balanced in sampler making. All this skill in lettering could be applied to the stores of household linen in the way of marking, for cross-stitch letters, done in colored threads, were a part of the finish of sheets and pillowcases and fine toweling which made so important a part of the riches of the household, and it led by easy grades of familiarity to more comprehensive methods of decoration. In truth, the letters first practiced in cross-stitch opened the door to all future elaborations, and were the vehicle of moral instruction as well; for little Puritans took their first doses of Bible history in carefully embroidered text, and their notions of pictorial art from cross-stitch illustrations. One finds upon some of the early examples pictures of Adam and Eve in the Garden of Eden, with the ever present author of sin, climbing the stem of the tree of life, or Jacob's dream of angels ascending and descending a ladder, [54] intersecting clouds of blue and smoke-colored stitches.

These pictorial samplers are certainly interesting, but those which confine themselves to simple cross-stitch with borders, and the name of the little child who wrought them, touch a note of domestic life which is more than interesting.

The sampler was purely English in its derivation and followed the English with great fidelity, although redolent of Puritan life and thought. Sometimes, indeed, it carried cross-stitch to the very limit of its capability in an attempt to render Bible scenes pictorially, but for the most part it was confined to the practice of various styles of lettering consolidated into text or verse.

The material upon which they were worked was generally of canvas, either white or yellow, and this was of English manufacture. As all manufactures were things of price, later samplers were often worked upon coarse homespun linens, which, barring the variations in the size of the threads inevitable in hand-spinning, made a fairly good material for cross-stitch.

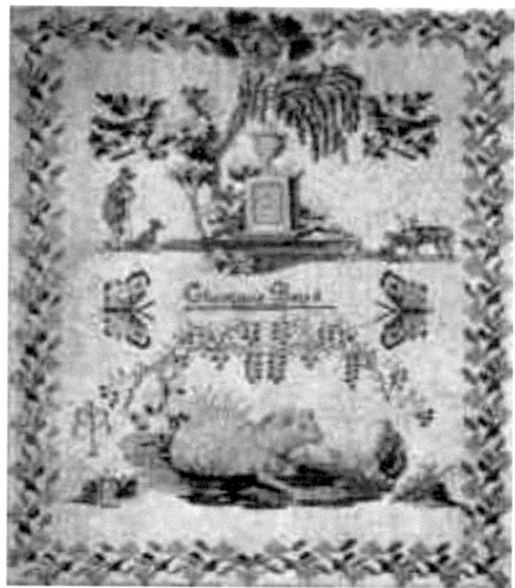

larger image

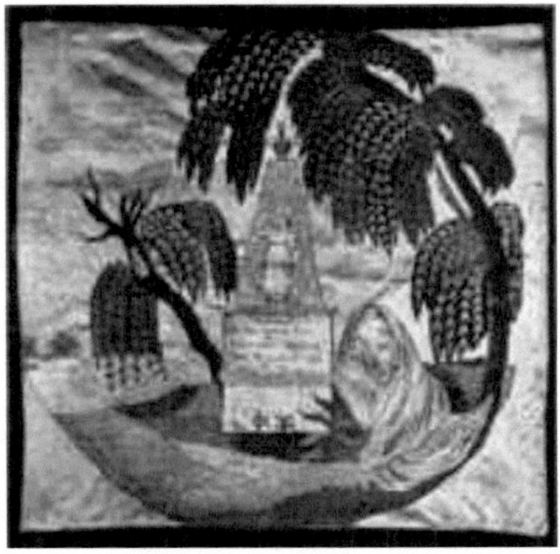

larger image

Courtesy of Essex Institute, Salem, Mass.

Left—SAMPLER worked by Christiana Baird. Late eighteenth century American.
Right—MEMORIAL PIECE worked in silks, on white satin. Sacred to the memory of Major Anthony Morse, who died March 22, 1805.

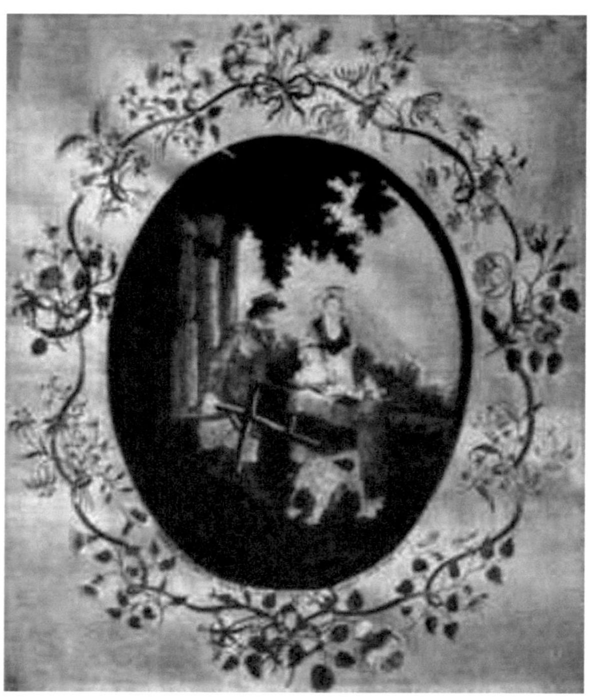

larger image

SAMPLER of Moravian embroidery, worked in 1806, by Sarah Ann Smith, of Smithtown, L. I.

Sampler making was a home rather than a school taught industry, going down from mother [55] to daughter along with darning and other processes of the needle, and having no relation, except that of its dexterity, to the distinct style of decorative embroidery called crewelwork, which accompanied it, or even preceded it.

The collecting of samplers has become rather a fad in these days, and as they are almost exclusively of New England origin, it gives an opportunity of acquaintance with the little Puritan girl which is not without its charm. As most of their samplers were signed with their names, the acquaintance becomes quite intimate, and one feels that these little Puritans were good as well as diligent. Here is Harmony Twitchell's name upon a blue and white sampler. What child whose name was Harmony could quarrel with other children, or

60

how could this other, whose long-suffering name was Patience, be resentful of the roughnesses of small male Puritans? Hate-evil and Wait-still and Hope-still and Thanks and Unity must have sat together like little doves and made crooked A's and B's and C's and picked out the frayed sewing-silk threads under the reproofs of the teacher of the Infant School, Miss Mather <u>or</u> Miss Coffin or Miss Hooker, whose father was [56] a clergyman, or even Miss Bradford, whose uncle was the Governor?

All this is in the story of the sampler, and so the teaching and practice of the canvas went constantly forward. The method was so simple, quite within the capacity of an alphabet-studying child. To make an A in cross-stitch was to create a link between the baby mind and the letter represented. There was no choice, no judgment or experience needed. The limit of every stitch was fixed by a cross thread, one little open space to send the needle down and another through which to bring it back, and the next one and the next, then to cross the threads and the thing was done. Yes, the little slips could make a sampler, every one of them, and when it was made, sometimes it was put in a frame with a glass over it, and Patience's mother would show it to visitors, and Patience would taste the sweets of superiority, than which there is nothing to the childish heart, nor even to mature humanity, so sweet.

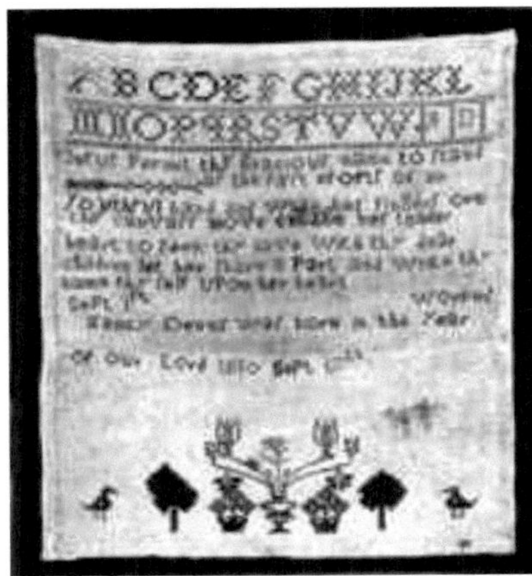

larger image

Courtesy Mrs. E. M. Sanford, Madison, N. J.

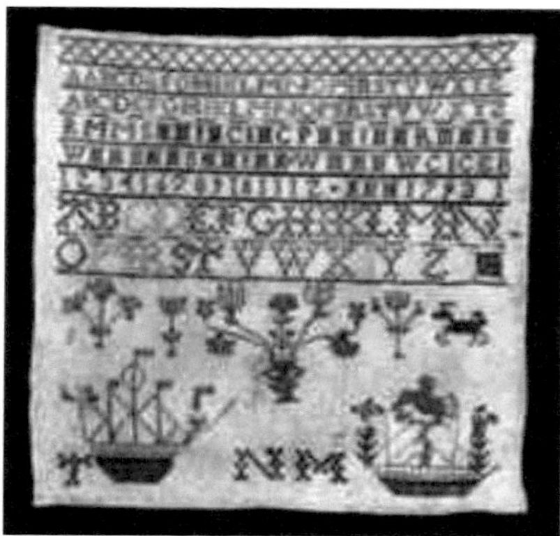

larger image

Courtesy Mrs. E. M. Sanford, Madison, N. J.

Left—SAMPLER worked by Nancy Dennis, Argyle, N. Y., in 1810.
Right—SAMPLER worked by Nancy McMurray, of Salem, N. Y., in 1793.

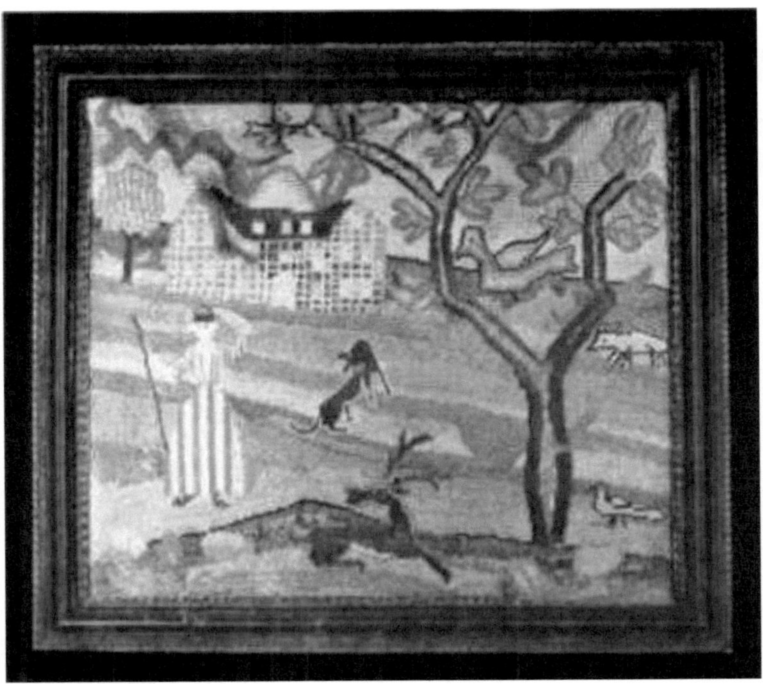

larger image

Courtesy Colonial Rooms, John Wanamaker, New York

PETIT POINT PICTURE which belonged to President John Quincy Adams, and now in the Dwight M. Prouty collection.

There were Infant Schools in my own days, little congregations of children not far removed from babyhood, who were taught the alphabet [57] from huge cards, and repeated it simultaneously from the great blackboard which was mounted in the center of the room. In the schools, as well as at home, every little girl-baby was taught to sew, to overhand minutely upon small blocks of calico, the edges turned over and basted together. When a perfect capacity for overhand sewing was established, the next short step was to the sampler, and the tiny fingers were guided along the intricacies of canvas crossings. The dear little rose-tipped fingers! the small hands! velvet soft and satin smooth, diverse even in their littlenesses! They were taught even then to be dexterous with woman's special tool, the very same in purpose and intent with which queens and dames and ladies had played long before.

The sampler world was a real world in those days, full of youth and as living as the youth of the world must always be, but now it is dead as the mummies, and the carefully preserved remains are only the shell which once held human rivalries and passions.

Quilts

The domestic needlework of the late seventeenth and early eighteenth centuries, should not [58] be overlooked in a history of embroidery, it being often so ambitiously decorative and the stitchery so remarkable. The patchwork quilt was an instance of much of this effort. It was unfortunate that an economic law governed this species of work, which prevented its possible development. The New England conscience, sworn to utility in every form, had ruled that no material should be *bought* for this purpose. It could only take advantage of what happened, and it seldom happened that cottons of two or three harmonious colors came together in sufficient quantity to complete the five-by-five or six-by-six which went to the making of a patchwork quilt. Nevertheless one sometimes comes across a "rising sun" or a "setting sun" bedquilt which is remarkable for skillful shading, and was an inspiration in the house where it was born, and where the needlework comes quite within the pale of ornamental stitchery.

This variety of domestic needlework, and one or two others which are akin to it, survived in the northern and middle states in the form of quilting until at least the middle of the nineteenth century, while in the southern states, especially in [59] the mountains of Kentucky and North Carolina, it still survives in its original painstaking excellence.

Among the earlier examples of these quilts one occasionally finds one which is really worthy of the careful preservation which it receives. I remember one which impressed itself upon my memory because of the humanity interwoven with it, as well as the skill of its making. It was a construction of blocks, according to patchwork law, every alternate block of the border having an applied rose cut from printed calico in alternate colors of yellow, red, and blue. These roses were carefully applied with buttonhole stitch, and the cotton ground underneath cut away to give uniform thickness for quilting. The main body of the quilt was unnoticeably good, being a collection of faintly colored patches of correct construction. The quilting was a marvel—a large carefully drawn design, evidently inspired by branching rose vines without flowers, only the leafage and stems being used, and all these bending forms filled in with a diamonded background of exquisite quilting. The palely colored center was distinguished only by its needlework, leaving the rose border to emphasize and frame it. [60]

There was a bit of personal history attached to this quilt in the shape of a small tag, which said:

"This quilt made by Delia Piper, for occupation after the death of an only son. Bolivar, Southern Missouri, 1845."

The same kind friend who had introduced me to this quilt, finding me appreciative of woman's efforts in fine stitchery, took me to call upon other pieces which were equally worthy of admiration. One was a white quilt of what was called "stuffed work," made by working two surfaces of cloth together, the upper one of fine cambric, the lower one of coarse homespun. Upon the upper one a large ornamental basket was drawn, filled with flowers of many kinds, the drawing outlines being followed by a back stitchery as regular and fine as if done by machine, looking, in fact, like a string of beaded stitches, and yet it was accomplished by a needle in the hand of a skillful but unprofessional sewer. The picture, for it was no less, was completed by the stuffing of each leaf and flower and stem with flakes of cotton pushed through the homespun lining. The weaving of the basket was a marvel of bands of buttonholed material, which stood out in appropriate thickness. [61] The centers of the flowers had simulated stamens done in knotted work.

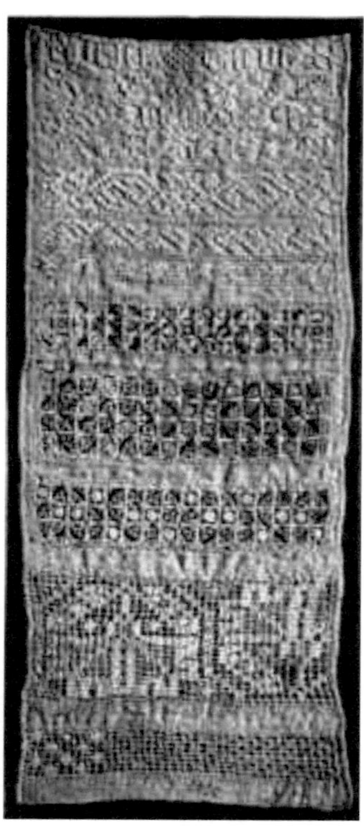

larger image

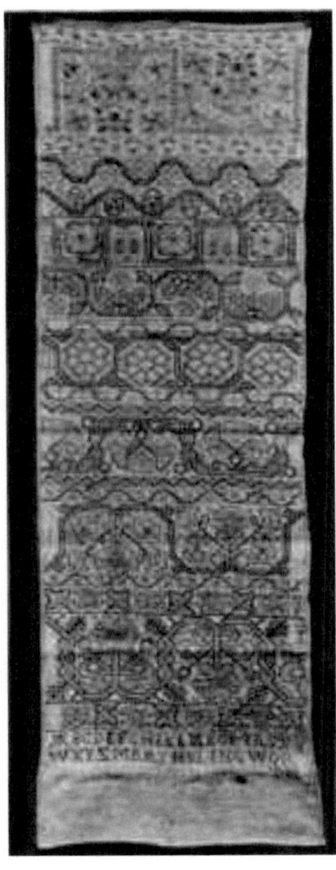

larger image

Courtesy of Essex Institute, Salem, Mass.

Left—SAMPLER in drawnwork, écru linen thread, made by Anne Gower, wife of Gov. John Endicott, before 1628.
Right—SAMPLER embroidered in dull colors on écru canvas by Mary Holingworth, wife of Philip English, Salem merchant, married July 1675, accused of witchcraft in 1692, but escaped to New York. *From the Curwen estate.*

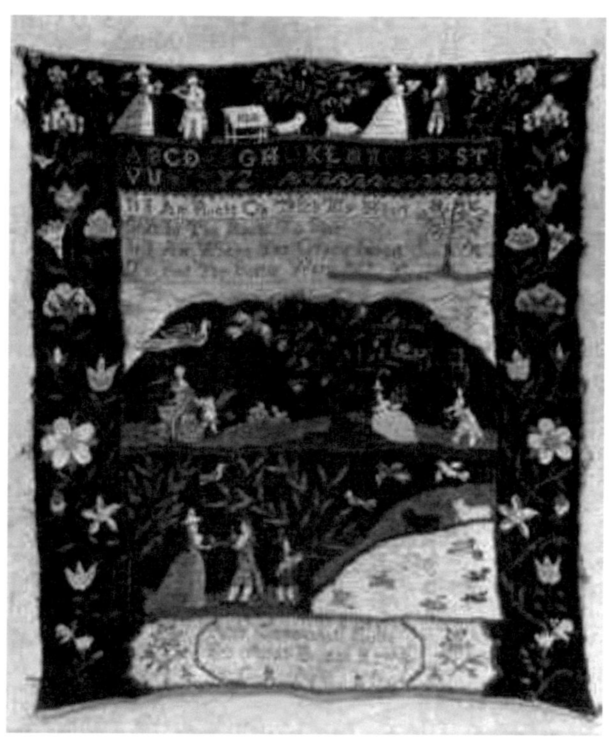

larger image

Courtesy Metropolitan Museum of Art

SAMPLER worked by Hattie Goodeshall, who was born February 19, 1780, in Bristol.

I think this stuffed work was rather rare, for I have only seen two specimens, and as it required unusual and exhaustive skill in needlework, the production was naturally limited. The practice was one of the exotic efforts of some one of large leisure and lively ambitions who belonged to the class of prosperous citizens.

"Patchwork," as it was appropriately called, was more often a farmhouse industry, which accounts for its narrow limits, since, with choice of material, even a small familiarity with geometrical design might bring good results. It might have easily become good domestic art. Geometrical borders in two colors would have taken

68

their place in decorative work, and the applied work, so often ventured upon, was the beginning of one very capable method. The skillful needlework, the elaborate quilting, the stitchery and stuffing are worthy of respect, for the foundation of it all was great dexterity in the use of the needle.

[62] CHAPTER IV MORAVIAN WORK, POR-TRAITURE, FRENCH EMBROIDERY, AND LACEWORK

While the ladies and house mistresses of New England were busy with their crewelwork, the children with their little samplers, and farm housemothers sewed patchwork in the intervals of spinning and weaving, an entirely different development of needlework art had taken place, beginning in Pennsylvania. Embroidery in America did not grow exclusively from seed brought over in the Mayflower. It sprang from many sources, but its finest qualities came from the influence of what was called "Bethlehem Embroidery."

The advent of this style of needlework was interesting. It originated in a religious community founded in 1722 at Herrnhut, Germany, by Count Zinzendorf. It was a strictly religious, semimonastic group of single men and single women, whose hearts were filled with zeal for mission work. At that period, I suppose America seemed a possible and promising field for such efforts, and accordingly forty-five of the brothers and as many of [63] the sisters turned their faces toward this new world. One can fancy that when the thought first entered their minds, of coming to a land peopled by savage Indians, with but a bare sprinkling of "the Lord's people," they trembled even in their dreams at the thought of the cruel incidents they might encounter in that wilderness toward which they were impelled by apostolic zeal, and the unquiet sea upon which they were about to embark foreshadowed an unknown future. But there was small danger for them upon the sea; surely they could not sink in troubled waters, these etherial souls! The heavenly quality of them would upbear the vessel and cargo. They would come safe to land, no matter how tempestuous the elements!

I suppose, at all periods of the world, prophet and martyr stuff might be sifted out from the man-stuff of the times if the race had need of them. In normal states of growth, we call them "cranks" and look for no results from their existence. But the elusive spirit of love never dies. It appears and reappears in the history of all races and

71

times, and leaves its mark upon them in various shapes of beneficence. [64]

These missionary brothers and sisters had chosen as the theater of
their labor that part of our broad land which was pleasantly chris-
tened Pennsylvania, and selecting a portion of the southern area,
they founded their colony and called it "Ephrata."

It existed for forty years, constantly increasing its membership,
and living a life reaching out toward a perfection of goodness which
seemed quite possible to their apostolic souls.

Time, however, brought changes of circumstance and of mind,
and after many philanthropic phases, in 1749 the mingled elements
and aspirations of the enlarged congregation were merged into two
boarding schools, one for boys, which was the germ of Lehigh University, and another for girls at Bethlehem, which, under the careful
fostering of the sisters, became the birthplace of the famous Moravian needlework. So were melted into the modern form of scholastic
instruction the various efforts of religious activity, the eternal reaching out for conditions in human life in which it is easy and natural
to be good and happy. It had not been accomplished in this semimonastic life, but the efforts toward it had their influence, [65] and,
you may judge by the quality of its founders, had never died.

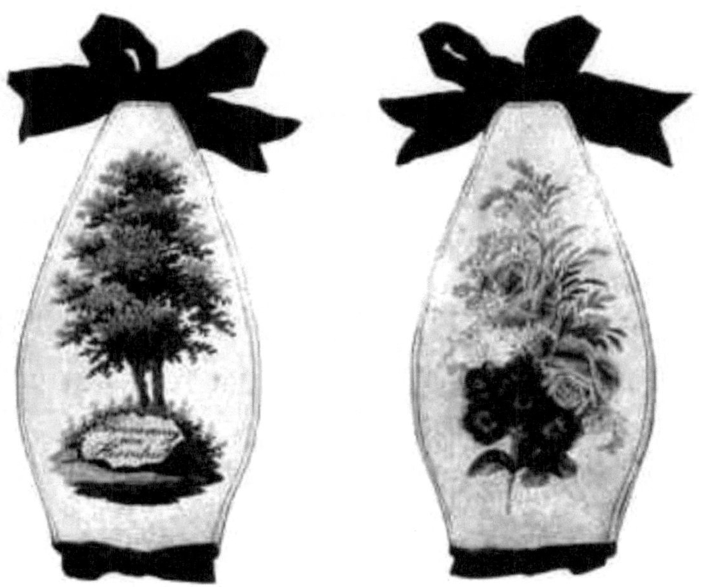

larger image

NEEDLEBOOK of Moravian embroidery, made about 1850. *Now in the possession of Mrs. J. U. Myers, Bethlehem, Pa.*

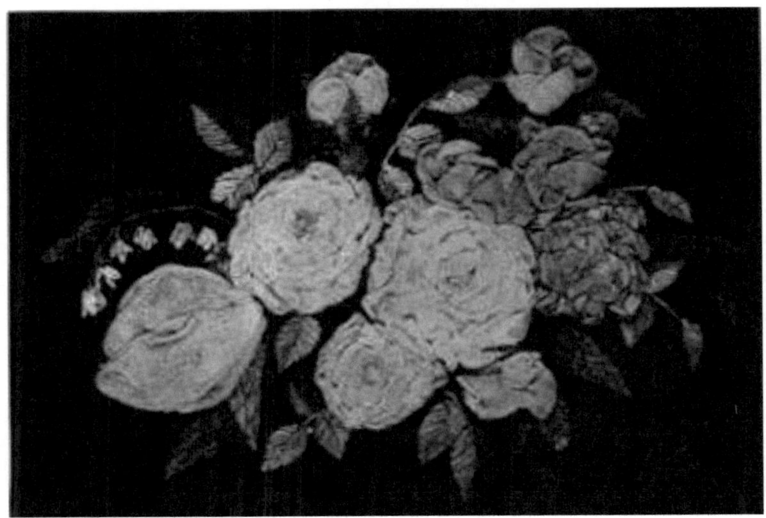

larger image

Courtesy of Claire Reynolds Tubbs, Gladstone, N. J.

MORAVIAN EMBROIDERY worked by Emily E. Reynolds, Plymouth, Pa., in 1834, at the age of twelve, while at the Moravian Seminary in Bethlehem, and now owned by her granddaughter.

The two schools very early in their history seem to have established a reputation for learning and culture which made them a desirable influence in the formative lives of the children of the most thoughtful, as well as the most prominent and prosperous, American families. Indeed, the school for girls became so popular as to lead to an extension and founding of several branches in other of the southern states. The art and practice of fine needlework became a popular and necessary feature of them, distinguishing them from all other schools. "Tambour and fine needlework" were among the extras of the school, and charged for, as we learn from school records, at the rate of "seventeen shillings and sixpence, Pennsylvania currency."

It was not alone tambour and fine needlework, as we shall see later, that was taught by the Moravian Sisters, but the ribbon work, crêpe work, and flower embroidery, and picture production upon satin. These pictures, however important as performances, were not the most common form of needlework taught by the [66] Sisters. Flower embroidery was the usual form of practice, and it was of a quality which made each one a wonder of execution and skill. The materials were satin of a superb quality for the background, or Eastern silk of softness and strength, and the silks used in the stitchery were generally "slack twisted" silk threads of very pure quality, and in certain cases, where they would not be likely to fray, lustrous flosses of Eastern make. The stitch used in these flower pieces was an over-and-over stitch, or what was called satin-stitch, which was without the lap of Kensington stitch. There was in every piece of embroidery done under the instruction of the accomplished and devoted Sisters certain virtues, certain effects of conscientious and patient work, mingled with the love of good and beautiful art, which were plainly visible. It had in all its flower pieces, and they were many, the quality of beautiful charm. The ministry of nature

may have had something to do with this, since the lives of the executants were open to its influences.

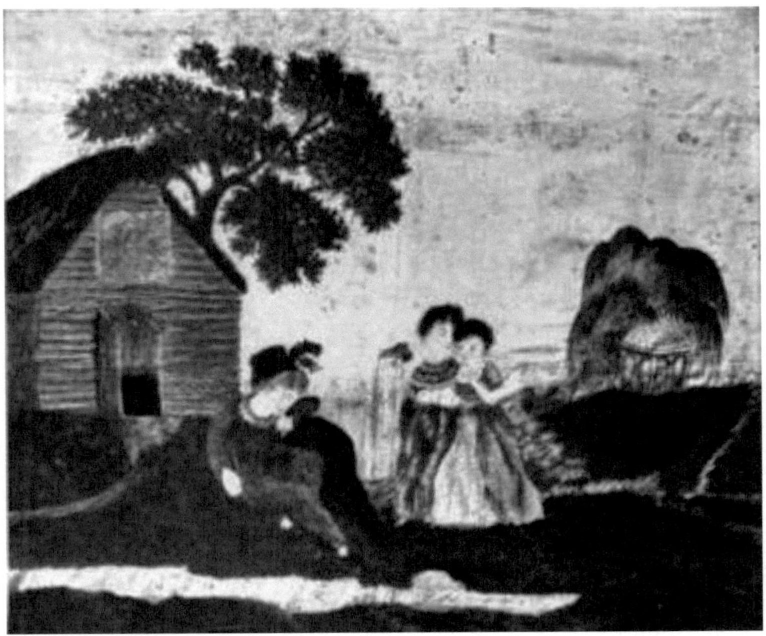

larger image

MORAVIAN EMBROIDERY from Louisville, Ky.

One can make a mental picture of those early days beside the
peaceful "Lehi," where the Sisters taught and nurtured the young
girls of [67] very young America, and trained them in such beautiful
and womanly accomplishments. The scattered bits of needlework
which remain to us are so fine, so clear, so thoroughly exhaustive of
all excellence in technique, that they are to the art of embroidery
what the ivory miniature is to painting. We cannot but hail the
memory of the Sisters of Bethlehem with respect and admiration.

I became familiar with the work of this community when I was
arranging an historic exhibition of American Embroidery for the
Bartholdi Fair in 1883. Few people may remember that, among the
means for the installation of the Bartholdi Statue of Liberty which
welcomes the world at the entrance to the harbor of New York, was

an effort called the Bartholdi Fair, held in the then almost new and very popular Academy of Design at the northwestern corner of Fourth Avenue and Twenty-third Street. Knowing the value of Bethlehem work, I made an effort to secure a representative collection, with the result of gathering a most interesting group of specimens, mainly by the interest and help of Mr. Henry Baldwin of Lehigh University, to whom I was referred for assistance in my purpose. I have [68] before me now the correspondence which ensued, a most painstaking, kind and patient one on his part, giving me much interesting history of the Bethlehem mission, as well as its life and progress. Among the legends is one — that during our Revolutionary war, Pulaski recruited some of his Legion at Bethlehem, and ordered a banner, which was carried by his troops until he fell in the attack upon Savannah. This banner is now in the rooms of the Maryland Historical Society, and I find the question of its having been an order from Count Pulaski, or a gift to the Legion, is one of very lively interest in the community.

This exhibit of 1883 was as complete an historical collection of American needlework as was possible, and I have a list of ten articles loaned from collections in Bethlehem, which reads as follows:

1. Embroidered pocketbook of black silk with flowers in bright colors. Former property of Bishop Bigler.
2. Embroidered needlebook of white satin with bright flowers, date 1800.
3. Embroidered needlebook of white satin with bright flowers and vines, dated 1786. [69]
4. Sampler, dated 1740.
5. Yellow velvet bag embroidered with ribbon work.
6. Black velvet bag embroidered in crêpe work with flowers.
7. White satin workbag embroidered in fine tracery of vines.
8. A box with embroidered pincushion on top.
9. A blue silk pocketbook with very fine ribbon work.
10. A paper box done with needle in filigree.

It will be seen by this list how varied were the forms of needlework taught at Bethlehem. The crêpe work mentioned in No. 6 is, probably owing to the perishable character of its material, very rare, but was extremely beautiful in effect. Bits of colored crêpe were gathered into flower petals and sewed upon satin, roses laid leaf upon leaf and built up to a charming perfection, while the stems and foliage were partially or wholly embroidered in silk.

The ribbon embroidery of No. 5, has been revived by the New York Society of Decorative Art and practiced with great success. The flower embroideries, in the specimens exhibited, [70] were of two sorts—the small groups being done with fine twisted silks in a simple "over and over" stitch, called at that time "satin stitch," alike on both sides, except that on the right side the flowers and leaves were raised from the surface by an under thread of cotton floss called "stuffing." This did not prevent, as it might easily have done, an unvarying regularity and smoothness, which was like satin itself, thread laid beside thread as if it were woven instead of sewed.

In the larger flowers, the sewing silk had been split into flosses, or perhaps the prepared flosses were used in the "tent stitch," which is now known as "Kensington." The colors of all these specimens were as fresh as natural flowers, speaking eloquently in praise of early processes of dyeing.

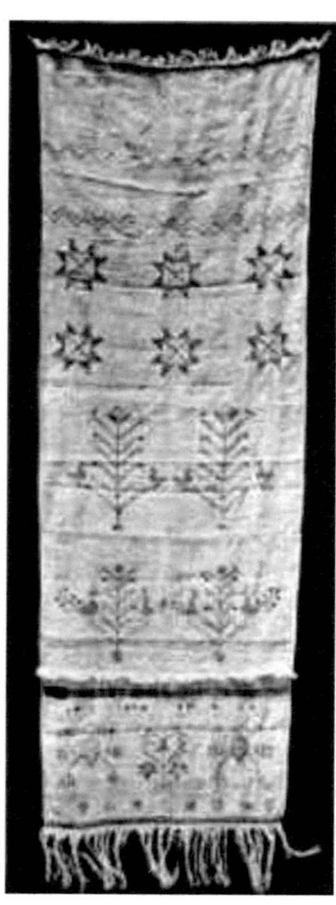

larger image

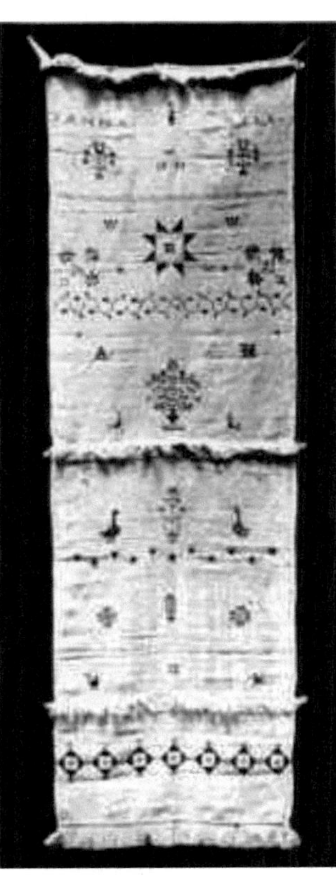

larger image

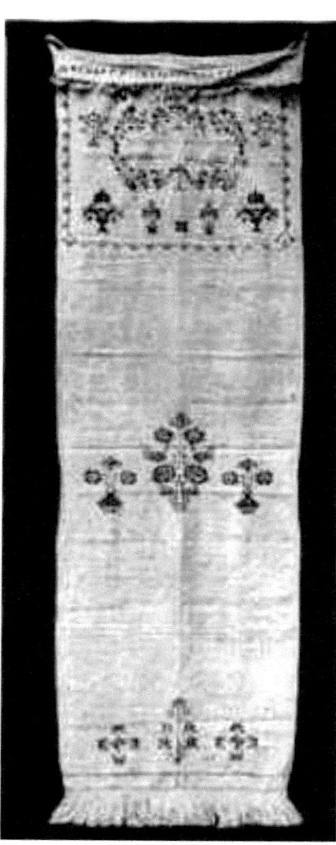

larger image

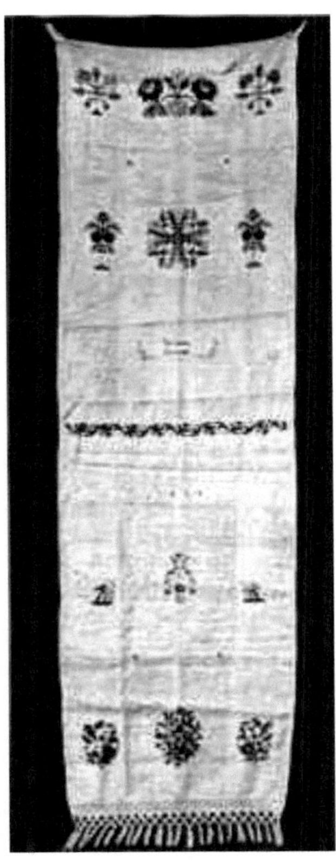

larger image

Courtesy Metropolitan Museum of Art

LINEN TOWELS embroidered in cross-stitch. Pennsylvania Dutch early nineteenth century.

These things seem to fairly exhale gentility, that quality-compact of everything superior in the life of early American womanhood. I have especially in mind one cushion where flowers, apparently as fresh in color as when the cushion was young, are laid upon a ground of silk of the pinky-ash color, once known as "ashes of roses." [71] The real charm of the thing, that which lends it a tender romance, is the legend worked upon the back of the cushion in brown silk stitches which are easily mistaken for the round-hand copperplate writing of the period—"Wrought where the peaceful

Lehi flows." One seems to breathe the very air of the secluded val-
ley, peopled by brethren and sisters set apart from the strenuous
duties of the builders of a new nation, and distinguished for learned
and devoted effort toward the perfection of moral, and spiritual,
rather than the conquests of material, life.

The Sisters had many orders from the outside world, as well as
from visitors, and the profit upon these helped to maintain the
school. Many of these orders were in the shape of pocketbooks,
pincushions, bags, etc., having a bunch, or wreath, or cluster of
flowers on one side, wonderfully wrought in silken flosses or sewing silks, and on the other, some pretty sentiment or legend done in
dark brown floss in the most perfect of "round-hand"; so perfect, in
fact, that it would require the closest scrutiny to decide that it was
not handwritten script.

These plentiful orders for things were induced [72] by the several
attractions of the situation, the remoteness from warlike and political disturbances, and the relationship of so many young girl lives, as
well as the interest which attached to the school and community,
making a constant demand in the shape of small articles of use or
luxury, decorated by the skillful fingers of the Sisters.

Parallel with this fine practice of flower embroidery, was a period
of far more important needlework, which we may call Picture Embroidery. This also owed its introduction to the Moravian School of
Bethlehem, although it was probably of early English origin, going
back to that period when English embroidery was the wonder of the
world; and the *opus plumarium*, or feather-pen stitch, or tent stitch,
or Kensington stitch, as it has been known in succeeding ages, first
attracted attention as a medium of art.

Passing from England to Germany it became purely ecclesiastical,
and even now one occasionally finds in Germany, and less often in
England, bits of ecclesiastical embroidery of unimaginable fineness,
commemorating Christ's miracles and other incidents of Bible history. [73] I know of one small specimen of ancient English art, covering a space of five by seven inches, where the whole Garden of
Eden with its weighty tragedy is represented by inch-long figures of
Adam and Eve, and a man-headed snake, discussing amicably the
advantages of eating or not eating the forbidden fruit.

Such elaboration in miniature embroidery made good the claim of English needlework to its first place in the world, since nothing more wonderful had or has been produced in the whole long history of needlework art. It was undoubtedly from this school, filtered through generations of secular practice, that the Moravian picture embroidery came to be a general American inheritance.

To adapt this wonderful method to the uses of social life was an admirable achievement, and whether by the sisters of the Moravian school, or the growth of pre-American influence and time, we do not certainly know, the fact remains, however, that it was here so cunningly adapted to the circumstances and spirit of colonial and early American days as to seem to belong entirely to them, and it would seem quite clear that Bethlehem [74] was the source of the most skillful needlework art in America. It was there that the fine ladies of the late eighteenth and early nineteenth centuries, who sat at the embroidery frame in the intervals when they were not "sitting at the harp," acquired their skill.

It was the romantic period of embroidery that makes a very telling contrast to the earlier crewel and later muslin embroidery of the New England states. The pieces were seldom larger than eighteen or twenty inches square, the size probably governed by the width of the superb satin which was so often used as a background. Not invariably, however, for I have seen one or two pieces worked upon gray linen where the surface was entirely covered by stitchery, landscape, trees, and sky showing an unbroken surface of satiny texture. Pictures from Bible subjects are frequent, and these have the air of having been copied from prints; in fact, I have seen some where the print appears underneath the stitches, showing that it was used as a design. These Scripture pieces seem to have employed a lower degree of talent than those having original design, and were probably the somewhat perfunctory [75] work of young girls whose interests were elsewhere. One picture which I have seen was treasured as a record of a very romantic elopement—the lover in the case, riding gayly away with his beloved sitting on a pillion behind him, and no witnesses to the deed but a small sister, standing at the gate of the homestead with outstretched hands and staring eyes.

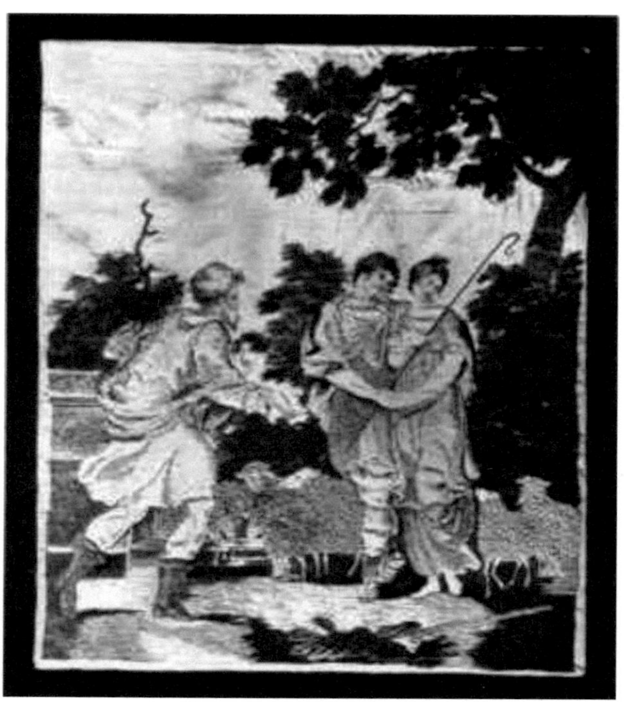

larger image

Courtesy of Elizabeth Lehman Myers

"THE MEETING OF ISAAC AND REBECCA"—Moravian embroidered picture, an heirloom in the Reichel family of Bethlehem, Pa. Worked by Sarah Kummer about 1790.

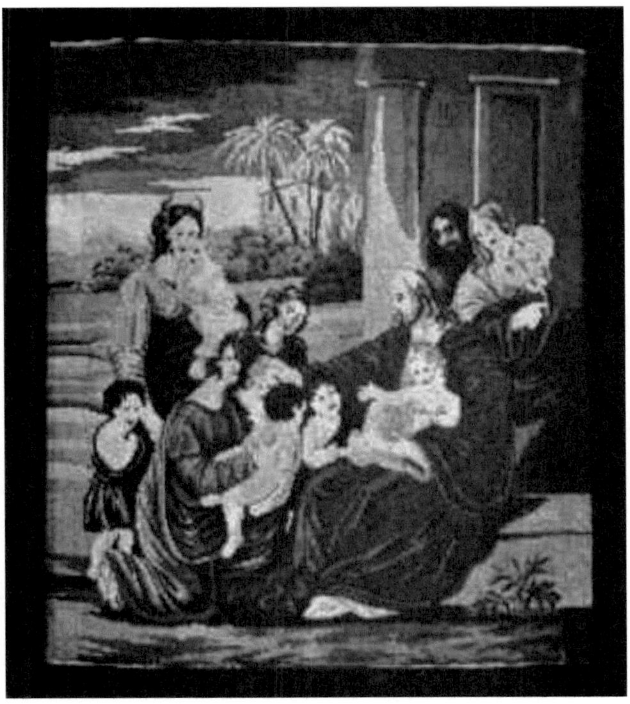

larger image

Courtesy of Elizabeth Lehman Myers

"SUFFER LITTLE CHILDREN TO COME UNTO ME"—Cross-stitch picture made about 1825, now in the possession of the Beckel family, Bethlehem, Pa.

The most important picture which I have seen in portrait needle-work came to light at the Baltimore Exhibition, and was a piazza group of five figures, a burly sea-captain seated in a rocking chair in a nautical dress and his own grayish hair embroidered above his ruddy face, his wife in a white satin gown seated beside him, and his three daughters of appropriately different ages grouped around, while the ship *Constance* was tied closely to the edge of the blue water which bordered the foreground of the picture. The composition of this picture was evidently the work of some experienced artist, for its incongruous elements kept their places and did not greatly clash. Taken as a whole it was an astonishing performance, quite too ambitious in its grasp for the novel art of needlework, and yet a thing to delight [76] the hearts of the descendants, or even casual possessors.

The Moravian teaching and practice spread the principles of needlework art so widely that it developed in many different directions. The wonderful silk embroidery applied to flowers was, like the arts of drawing and painting, capable of being used in copying all forms of beauty. It was sometimes, not always, successfully applied to landscape representation, and grew at last into a scheme of needlework portraiture, in this form perpetuating family history. It was sometimes used in conjunction with painting, the faces of a family group being done in water color upon cardboard by professional painters who were members of the art guild, who wandered from one social circle to another, supplying the wants of embroideresses ambitious of distinction in their accomplishments. The small painted faces were cut from the cardboard upon which they had been painted and worked around, often with the actual hair of the original of the portrait. I have seen one picture of a Southern beauty, where the golden hair had been wound into tiny curls, and sewn into place, and the lace of the neckwear [77] was so cleverly simulated as to look almost detachable. Of course such pictures were the result of individual experiment on the part of some very able and ambitious needlewoman.

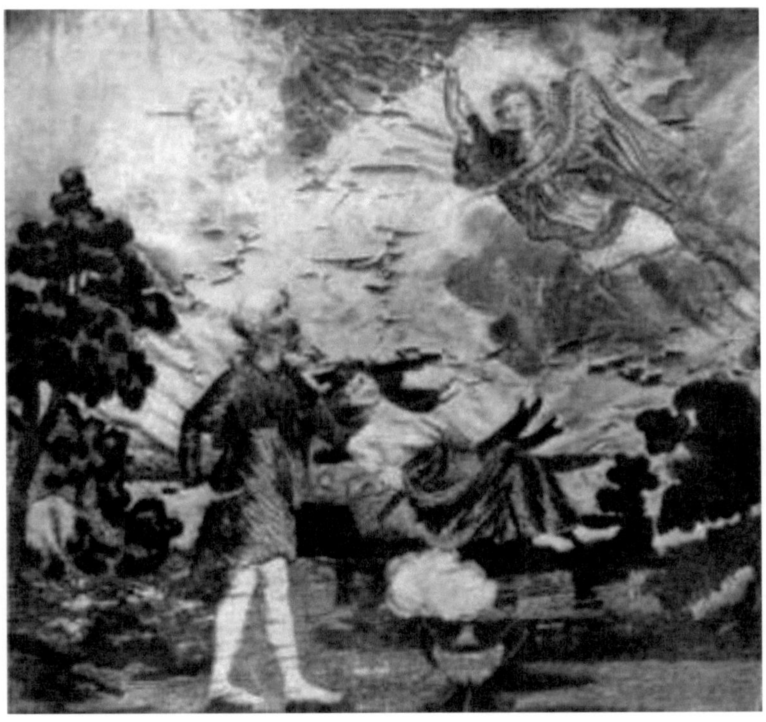

larger image

Courtesy of Mrs. R. B. Mitchell, Madison, N. J.

ABRAHAM AND ISAAC. Kensington embroidery by Mary Winifred Hoskins of Edenton, N. C., while attending an English finishing school in Baltimore in 1814.

One can imagine that the effect of them in social life was to add greatly to the vogue of the art of needlework. The most numerous of these relics were called "mourning pieces"—bits of memorial embroidery—the subject of the picture being generally a monument surmounted by an urn, overhung with the sweeping branches of a willow, while standing beside the monument is a weeping female figure, the face discreetly hidden in a pocket handkerchief. The inscriptions, "Sacred to the memory," etc., were written or printed upon the satin in India ink, and often the letters of the name were worked with the hair of the subject of the memorial.

In these pieces it is rather noticeable that the mourning figure is always draped in white, which leads to the conclusion that it is a purely emblematic figure of an emotion, rather than a real mourner. The shading of the monument was generally done in India ink, so that the actual embroidery was confined to the trunk and long [78] branches of weeping willow, and the dress of the figure, and the ground upon which willow and monument and figure stand. The faces being always hidden by the handkerchief, and a tinted satin serving for the sky, the execution of these memorial pictures was comparatively simple. They certainly bear an undue proportion to those happy family portraits where mother and children, or husband and wife, sit in love and simplicity before the pillared magnificence of the family mansion.

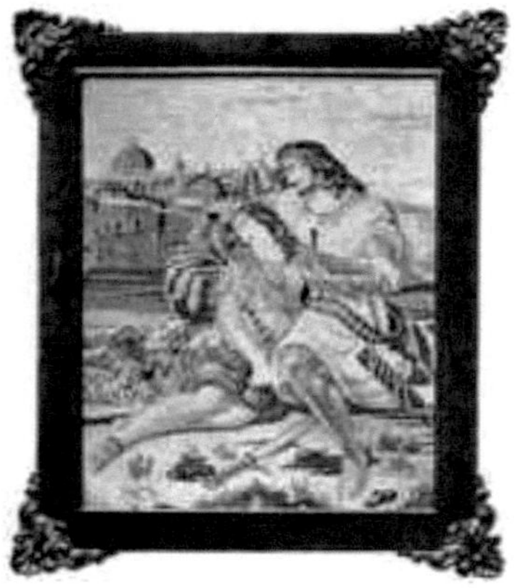

larger image

Courtesy of Essex Institute, Salem, Mass.

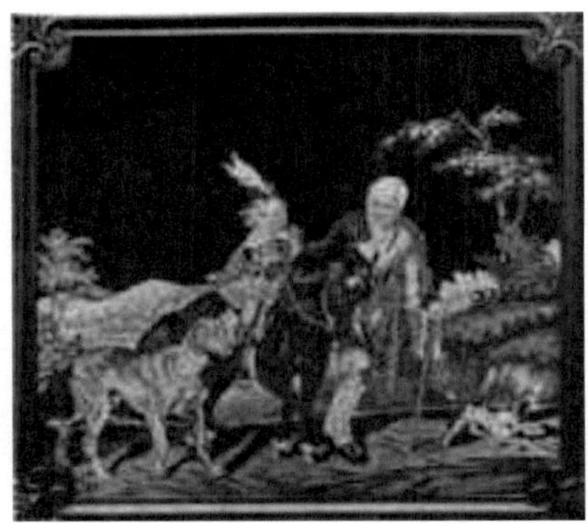

larger image

Courtesy of Essex Institute, Salem, Mass.

Left—FIRE SCREEN embroidered in cross-stitch worsted. *From the McMullan family of Salem.*

Right—FIRE SCREEN, design, "The Scottish Chieftain," embroidered in cross-stitch by Mrs. Mary H. Cleveland Allen.

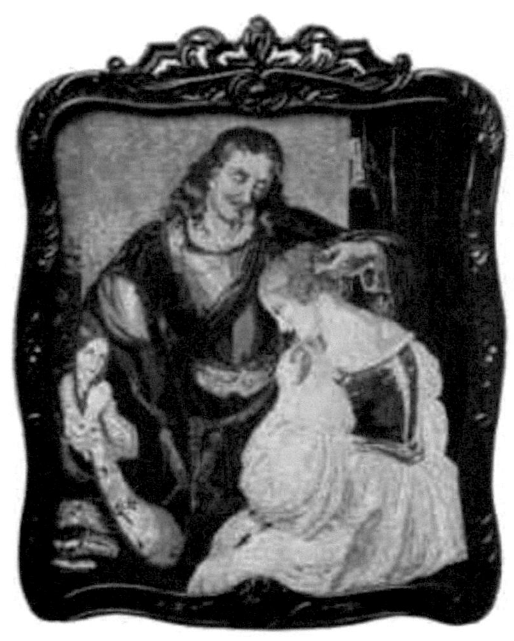

larger image

FIRE SCREEN worked about 1850 by Miss C. A. Granger, of Canandaigua, N. Y.

Perhaps the greater simplicity and ease of execution of the mourning pieces had something to do with their greater number. They may have been the first spelling of the difficult art of pictorial embroidery. The best of these picture embroideries were certainly wonderful creations as far as the use of the needle was concerned, and I fancy were done in the large leisure of some colonial home where early distinction in the art of needlework must have gone hand in hand with the skill of the traveling portrait painter. These dainty productions, with their delicately painted faces and hands, are far more often found than those with embroidered flesh. In some of these, [79] faces painted with real miniature skill upon bits of parchment have been inserted or superimposed upon the satin, the edges, as I have said, carefully covered by embroidery, done with single hair threaded into the needle instead of silk. In one case

90

which I remember, the yellow hair of a child was knotted into a bunch of solid looking curls covering the head of a small figure, while the face of the mother was surmounted by bands of a reddish brown. This little touch of realism gave a curious note of pathos to the picture of a life separated from the present by time and outgrown habits, but linked to it by this one tangible proof of actual existence.

The drawing or plan of these pictures was evidently done directly upon the satin ground, as one often finds the outlines showing at the edge of the stitches; but in the few specimens I have found where they were worked upon linen it had been covered with a tracing on strong thin paper, and the entire design worked through and over both paper and canvas. Those which were done upon linen seemed to belong to an earlier period than those worked on satin, which was perhaps an American adaptation of the [80] earlier method. Certainly the soft thick India satin, which was the ground of so many of them, made a delightful surface for embroidery, and blended with its colors into a silvery mass where work and background were equally effective. Two of these have survived the century or more of careful seclusion which followed the proud éclat of their production. One of the fortunate heirs to many of these exhibited treasures told me of a package or book containing heads in water color, evidently to be used as copies for the faces which might be found necessary for efforts in embroidery. The painting of these was perhaps a part of the education or accomplishment considered necessary to girls of prominent and successful families of the day.

Under favorable circumstances, such as a convenient relation between artist and needlework, this art would have developed into needlework tapestry. The groups would have outgrown their frames, and left their picture spaces on the walls, and, stretching into life-size figures, have become hangings of silken broidery, such as we find in Spain and Italy, from the hands of nuns or noble ladies.

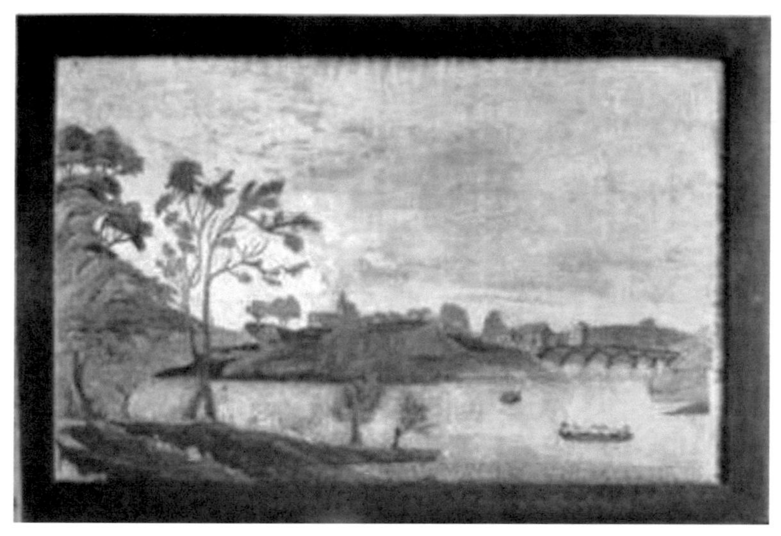

larger image

Courtesy of Essex Institute, Salem, Mass.

EMBROIDERED PICTURE in silks, with a painted sky.

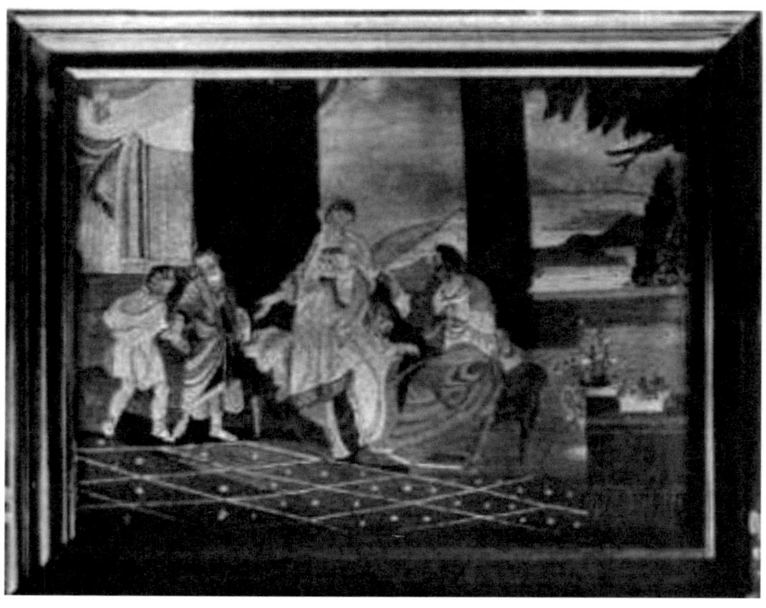

larger image

Courtesy of Essex Institute, Salem, Mass.

CORNELIA AND THE GRACCHI. Embroidered picture in silks, with velvet inlaid, worked by Mrs. Lydia Very of Salem at the age of sixteen while at Mrs. Peabody's school.

[81] The influence of the Bethlehem teaching lasted long enough to build up a very fine and critical standard of embroidery in America. It would be difficult to overestimate the importance of the influence of this school of embroidery upon the needlework practice of a growing country. Its qualities of sincerity, earnestness, and respect for the art of needlework gave importance to the work of hands other than that of necessary labor, and these qualities influenced all the various forms of work which followed it. The first divergence from the original work was in its application, rather than its method, for instead of having a strictly decorative purpose its application became almost exclusively personal. Flower embroidery of surpassing excellence was its general feature. The materials for the development of this form of art were usually satin, or the flexible undressed India silk which lent itself so perfectly to ornamentation. Breadths of cream-white satin, of a thickness and softness almost unknown in the present day, were stretched in Chippendale embroidery frames, and loops and garlands of flowers of every shape and hue were embroidered upon them. They were often done for skirts and sleeves [82] of gowns of ceremony, giving a distinction even beyond the flowered brocades so much coveted by colonial belles.

This beautiful flower embroidery was, like its predecessor, the rare picture embroidery, too exacting in its character to be universal. It needed money without stint for its materials, and luxurious surroundings for its practice. Some of the beautiful old gowns wrought in that day are still to be seen in colonial exhibitions, and are even occasionally worn by great-great-granddaughters at important mimic colonial functions.

Floss embroidery upon silk and satin was not entirely confined to apparel, for we find an occasional piece as the front panel of one of the large, carved fire screens, which at that date were universally used in drawing-rooms as a shelter from the glare and heat of the great open fires which were the only method of heating. As the back of the screen was turned to the fire and the embroidered face to the room, its decoration was shown to admirable advantage, and one can hardly account for the rarity of the specimens of these antique screens, except upon the supposition that the roses, carnations, and forget-me-nots [83] were still more effective when wrought upon the scant skirt of a colonial gown, instead of being shrouded in their careful coverings in the deserted drawing-room, and my lady of the embroidery might more effectively exhibit them in the lights of a ballroom. In recording the changes in the style and purposes of embroidery, from the days of homespun and home-dyed crewel to the almost living flowers wrought with lustrous flosses upon breadths of satin which were the best of the world's manufacture, one unconsciously traverses the ground of domestic and political history, from the days of the Pilgrims to the pomp of colonial courts.

French Embroidery

The character and purposes of the art varied with every political and national change. In the middle of the eighteenth century, a demand had gone out from the new and growing America, and wandering over the seas had asked for something fine and airy with which to occupy delicate hands, unoccupied with household toil. The carefully acquired skill of the earlier periods of our history became in succeeding generations [84] almost an inheritance of facility, and easily merged into the elaborate stitchery called French embroidery. I can find no trace of its having been *taught*, but plenty of proofs of its existence are to be seen on the needlework pictures under glass still hanging in many an old-fashioned parlor, or relegated to the curiosity corner of modern drawing-rooms. It is possible that the close intimacy existing between France and England at that period may have influenced this art. Many French families of high degree were seeking safety or profit in this country, and the convent-bred ladies of such families would naturally have shared their acquirements with those whose favor and interest were important to them as strangers. There was another form of this French embroidery, the materials used being cambrics, linens, and muslins of all kinds, the most precious of which were the linen-cambrics and

India mulls. The use of the former still survives in the finest of French embroidered pocket handkerchiefs, but the latter is seldom seen except in the veils and vests of Oriental women, or in the studio draperies of all countries.

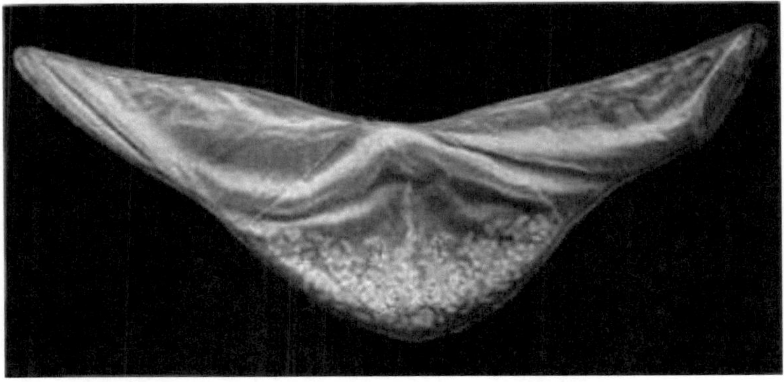

larger image

Courtesy Metropolitan Museum of Art, New York

CAPE of white lawn embroidered. Nineteenth century American.

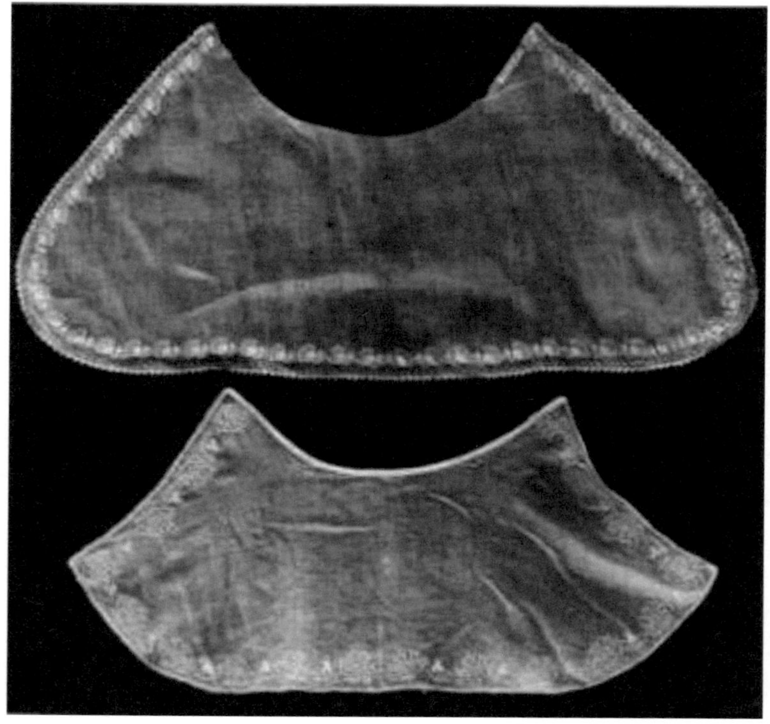

larger image

Courtesy Metropolitan Museum of Art, New York

COLLARS of white muslin embroidered. Nineteenth century American.

The threads used were flosses of linen or cotton, [85] preferably the latter, which were almost entirely imported. With these restricted materials, wonders of ornamentation were performed. The stitch, quite different from that of crewelwork or picture embroidery of the preceding period, was the simple over and over stitch we find in French embroidery of the present day. The leaves of the design or pattern were frequently brought into relief by a stuffing of under threads.

Everything was embroidered; gowns, from the belt to lower hem, finished with scalloped and sprigged ruffles in the same delicate workmanship, were everyday summer wear. Slips and sacques, which were not quite as much of an undertaking as an entire gown, were bordered and ruffled with the same embroidery. The amount and beauty of specimens which still exist after the lapse of nearly a century is quite wonderful. Small articles, like collars, capes and pelerines, were almost entirely covered with the most exquisite tracery of leaf and flower, a perfect frostwork of delicate stitchery, with patches of lacework introduced in spaces of the design.

The designs were seldom, almost never, original, being nearly always copied directly from what [86] was called "boughten work," to distinguish it from that which was produced at home.

Many beautiful and skillful stitches were used in this form of work. Lace stitches, made with bodkins or "piercers," or darning needles of sufficient size to make perforations, were skillfully rimmed and joined together in patterns by finer stitches, and open borders, and hemstitching, and dainty inventions of all kinds, for the embellishment of the fabrics upon which they were wrought.

With these materials and these methods most of the women of the different sections of the country busied themselves from a period beginning probably about 1710 and extending to 1840, and it is safe to say, notwithstanding the apparent simplicity of life between those dates, that at no period in the history of woman was as much time and consummate skill bestowed upon wearing apparel. Many a young girl of the day embroidered her own wedding dress, and during the months or years of its preparation suffered and enjoyed the same ambition which goes on in the present, to the acquirement of some wonder of French composition, or costly ornament of point lace and pearls.

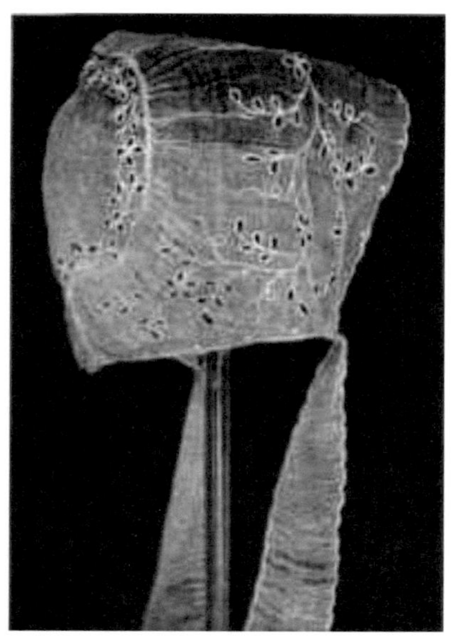

larger image

Courtesy Metropolitan Museum of Art

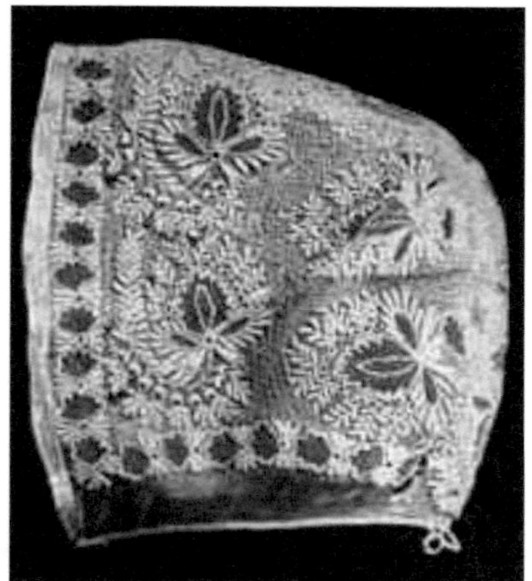

larger image

Courtesy Mrs. Isaac Pierson, Canandaigua, N. Y.

Left—BABY'S CAP White mull, with eyelet embroidery. Nineteenth century American.

Right—BABY'S CAP Embroidered mull. 1825.

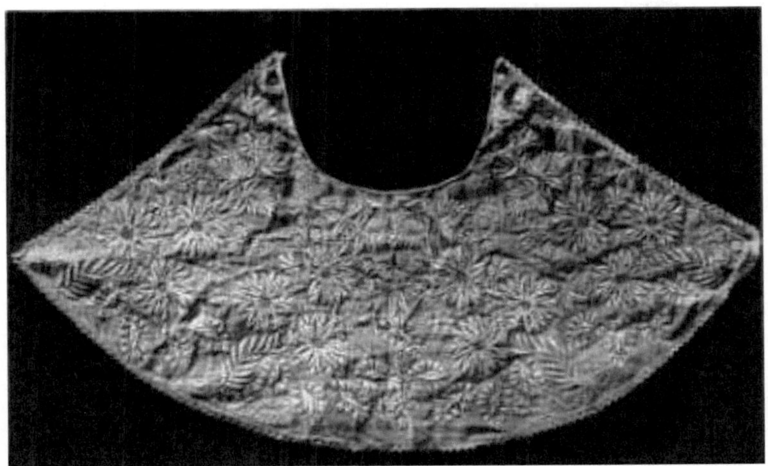

larger image

Courtesy Metropolitan Museum of Art

COLLAR of white embroidered muslin. Nineteenth century American.

[87] Everything was embroidered. The tender, downy head of the newly born baby was covered with a cap of delicatest material incrusted to hardness with needlework. The baby's caps of the period are a perfect chapter of human emotions; mother-love, emulation, pride, and declaration of family or personal position are skillfully expressed in a multiplicity of decorative stitches. A six-foot length of baptismal robe carried for half its length the same elaborate stitchery. Long delicate ruffles were edged with double rows of scallops. Double and triple collars and "pelerines" of muslin were to be found in the hands of all women of high or low degree. Articles of wearing apparel were done upon a soft fine muslin called mull, breadths of which were embroidered for skirts, lengths of it were scalloped and embroidered for flounces, and hand-lengths of it were done for the short waists and sleeves of the pretty Colonial gowns worn by our delicate ancestresses. One of these gowns,

stretched to its widest, would hardly cover a front breadth of the habit of one of our well-nurtured athletic girls of the present, and the athletic girl can show no such handiwork as this. [88]

Beautiful embroidery it was that was lavished upon muslin gowns, baby's caps and long, long robes, and upon aprons, pelerines and capes. Over stitch instead of tent stitch was the order of the day. "Tent stitch and the use of the globes" was no longer advertised as a part of school routine. Instead of this, there were the most delicate overstitches and multitudinous lace-stitches which we nowhere else find, unless in the finest of Asian embroidery.

A large part of the eighteenth and the first quarter of the nineteenth century was a period of remarkable skill in all kinds of stitchery. It was not confined to embroidery, but was also applied to all varieties of domestic needlework. Hemstitched ruffles were a part of masculine as well as feminine wear, and finely stitched and ruffled shirts for the head of the household were quite as necessary to the family dignity as embroidered gowns and caps for its feminine members.

It would be difficult to enumerate all the uses to which the national perfection of needle dexterity was put. It was, indeed, a national dexterity, for although its application was widely different in the eastern and southern states, the two schools of [89] needlework, as we may term them, met and mingled to a common practice of both methods in the middle states.

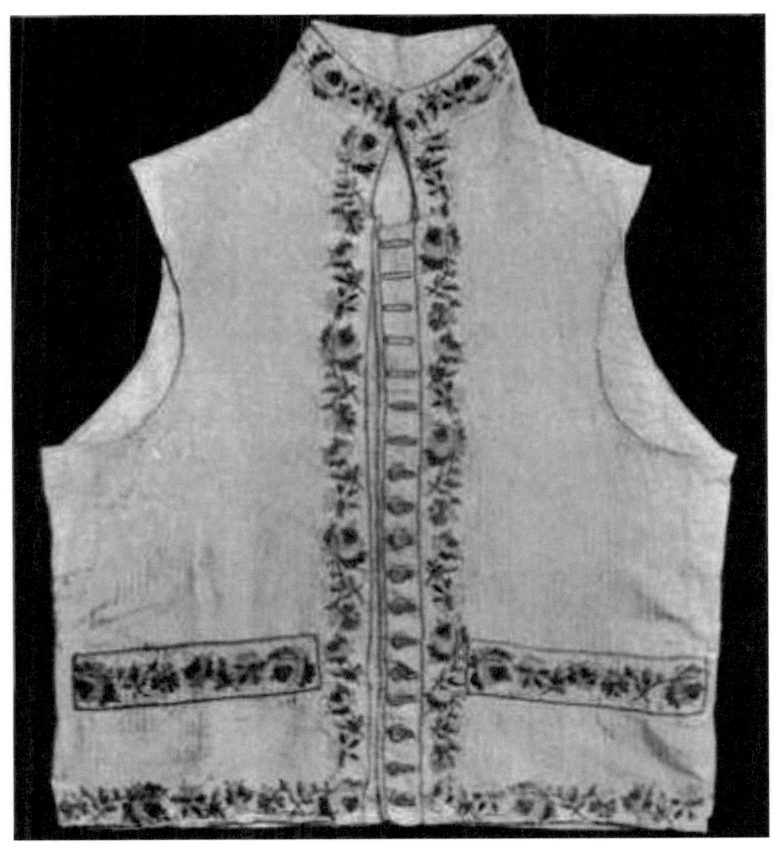

larger image

Courtesy of Bergen County Historical Society, Hackensack, N. J.

EMBROIDERED SILK WEDDING WAISTCOAT, 1829. From the Westervelt collection.

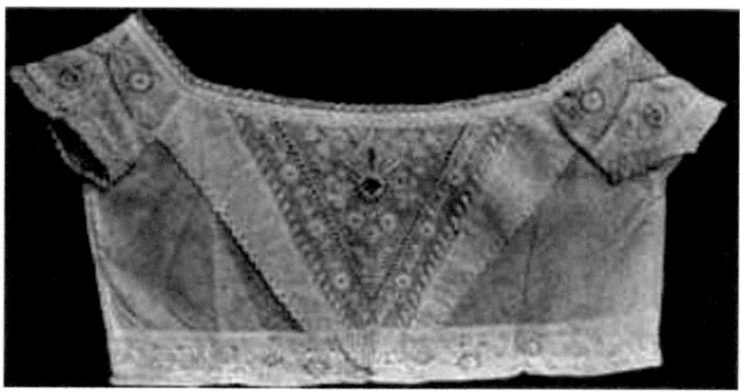

larger image

Courtesy of Bergen County Historical Society, Hackensack, N. J.

EMBROIDERED WAIST OF A BABY DRESS. 1850. From the collection of Mrs. George Coe.

Perhaps one may account for the prevalence of this kind of work, as it existed at a period of very limited education or literary pursuits among women. Domestic life was woman's kingdom, and needlework was one of its chief conditions. But whatever cause or causes stimulated the vogue of this variety of embroidery, we find it was universal among rich and poor, in city and country, for nearly three-quarters of a century. The narrow roll of muslin, for scalloped flounces and ruffling, and the skeins of French cotton went everywhere with girls and women, except to church and to ceremonious functions where men were included. Needlework was far more than an interest, it was an occupation.

The varieties of tambour work and open stitchery of various ornamental kinds were possible for all capacities. It was a general form of fine needlework, happily available to women of the farmhouse, as well as of the mansion, and its exceeding precision and beauty gave a character to the purely utilitarian stitchery of the day [90] which has made a high standard for succeeding generations. The hemstitched ruffles of shirts, the stitched plaits of simpler ones, the buttonholed triangles at the intersection of seams—all these practically unknown to modern construction—were probably the result of the skillful and careful needlework ornamentation of simple fabrics.

102

As an occupation, French embroidery practically displaced the making of cabinet pictures of graceful ladies in scant satin gowns which had occupied the embroidery frame, or decorated drawing-room walls. Flowers ceased to blossom upon pincushions, and the engrossing and prevalent occupation of needlework was entirely devoted to personal wear.

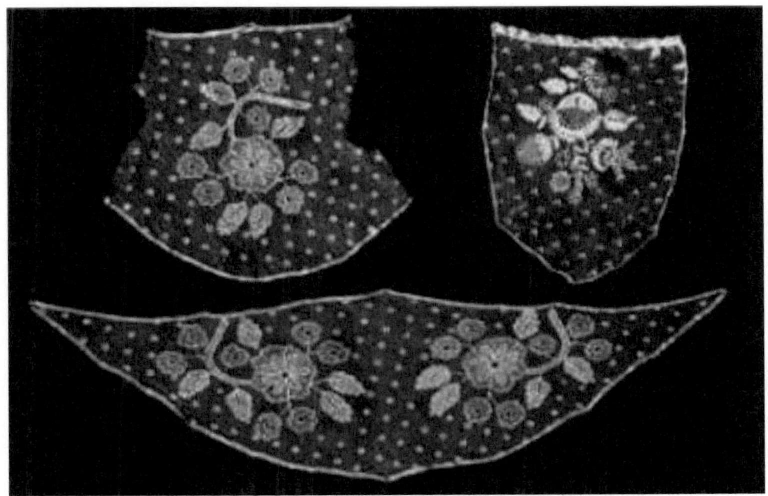

larger image

Courtesy of Mrs. A. S. Hewitt

EMBROIDERY ON NET. Border for the front of a cap made about 1820.

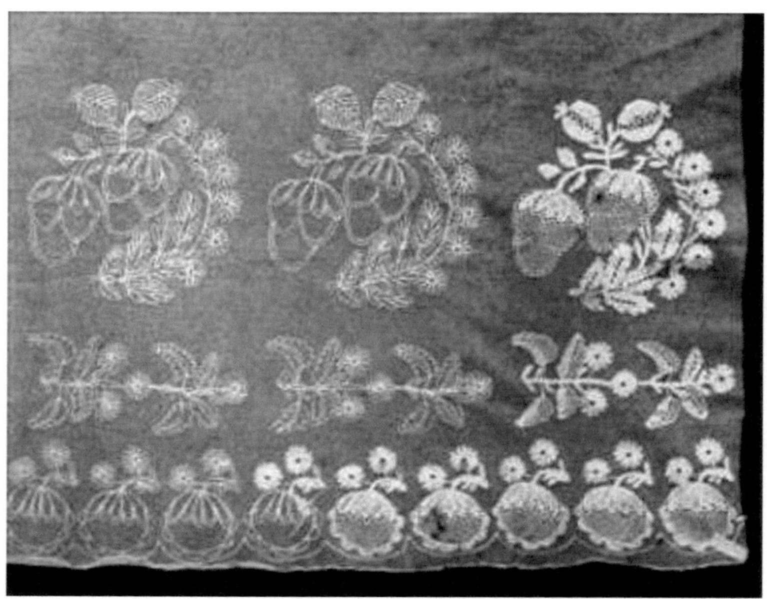

larger image

Courtesy of Metropolitan Museum of Art, New York

VEIL (unfinished) hand run on machine-made net. American nineteenth century.

At this period, however, ships were coming into Boston and other eastern ports almost daily or weekly, instead of at intervals of weary months. Ships were going to and returning from China and the Indies and the islands of the sea, laden on their return voyages not only with spices and liquors and sweets of the southern world, but with satins and velvets and silks and prints, and delicately printed muslins and cambrics; and the [91] fair linen and cotton flosses disappeared from the hands of needlewomen. Manufacturers had brought their looms to weave designs into the fabrics they produced and to simulate the work of the needle in a way which made one feel that the very spindles thought and wrought with conscious love of beauty.

The larger demands of luxurious living increased also the necessary work of the needle, and while the looms of France and Switzerland were busy weaving broidered stuffs, the needles of sewing women were kept at work fashioning the necessary garments of the millions of playing and working human beings. It was the era which gave birth to the "Song of the Shirt," a day of personal and exacting practice.

Lacework

The disappearance of the practice of French embroidery was as sudden as the dropping of a theater curtain, but a coexistent art called Spanish lacework lingered long after muslin embroidery had ceased to be. It was chiefly used in the elaboration of shawls, and large lace veils, which were a very graceful addition to Colonial [92] and early American costume. There is no difficulty in tracing this kind of decorative needlework. It came from Mexico into New Orleans, and from there, by various secrets of locomotion, spread along the southern states.

The veils were yard squares of delicate white or black lace, heavily bordered and lightly spotted with flowers, while the shawls were sometimes nearly double that size, and of much heavier lace, as they had need to be, to carry the wealth of decorative darning lavished upon them.

The design was always a foliated one, generally proceeding from a common center, representing a basket or a knot of ribbon, which confined the branching forms to the point of departure. The edges were heavily scalloped, with an extension of the ornamentation which included a rose or leaf for the filling of every scallop. The centers of flowers, and even of leaves, were often filled with beautiful variations of lace stitches worked into the meshes of the ground, and were very curious and interesting.

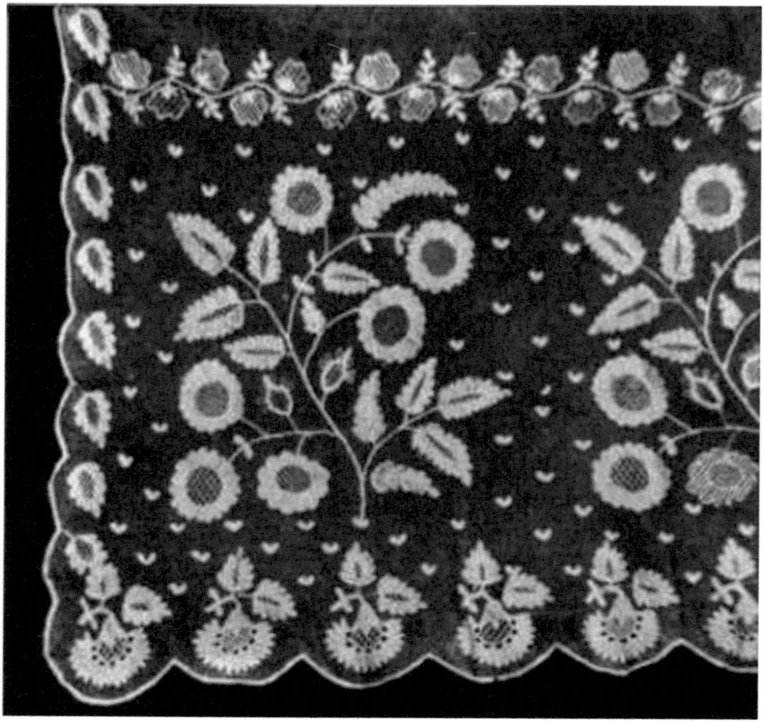

larger image

Courtesy of Bergen County Historical Society, Hackensack, N. J.

LACE WEDDING VEIL, 36 × 40 inches, used in 1806. From the collection of Mrs. Charles H. Lozier.

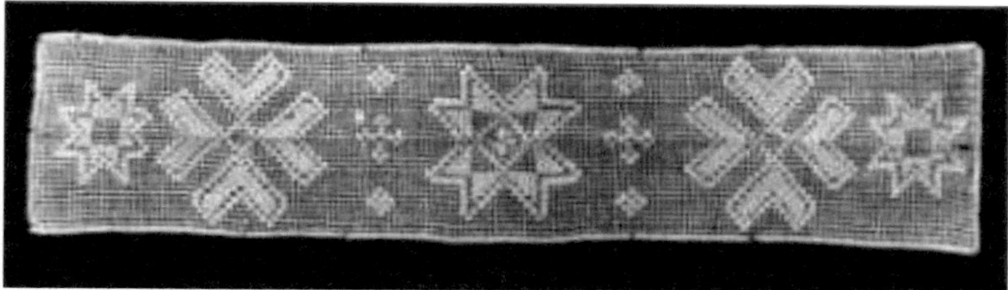

larger image

Courtesy of Bergen County Historical Society, Hackensack, N. J.

HOMESPUN LINEN NEEDLEWORK called "Benewacka" by the Dutch. The threads were drawn and then whipped into a net on which the design was darned with linen. Made about 1800 and used in the end of linen pillow cases.

Darning with flosses upon both white and black bobbinet, or silk net, was a very common [93] form of the art, and veils of white with seed or all-over designs darned in white silk floss, may be called the "personal needlework" of the period, and some of the shawls were superb stretches of design and stitching. This art, although so beautiful in effect, demanded very little of the skill necessary to the preceding methods of embroidery. The lace was simply stretched or basted over paper or white cloth, upon which the design was heavily traced in ink; the spaces which were to be solidly filled were sometimes covered with a shading of red chalk, and when this was done, it was a matter of simple running over and under the meshes of the net, in directions indicated by the shape of the leaf or flower. The work could be heavier or lighter, according to the design and size or weight of the flosses used. I have seen a wedding veil worked upon a beautiful white silk net, carrying a sprinkling of orange flowers, darned with white silk flosses, and a heavy wreath around the border. Certainly no veil of priceless point lace could be so etherially beautiful as was this relic of the past, and certainly no commercial product, however costly, could carry in its transparent folds the sentiment of [94] such a bridal veil, wrought in love by the bride who was to wear it.

I have seen one beautiful shawl, where the entire design was done in shining silver-white flosses, upon a ground of black net, with the effect of a disappearance of the background, the wreaths and groups of flowers seeming to float around the figure of the wearer.

In one or two instances, also, I have seen shawls in varicolored flosses producing a silvery mass of ornamentation which was most effective, but they were experiments which evidently did not commend themselves to North American taste.

The same method of darning was used upon what was then called, "bobbinet footing," narrow lengths of bobbinet lace which were extensively used as ruffles for caps and trimming and garniture of capes and various articles of personal wear.

Cap bodies were also worked in this method; in fact, the decorative treatment of caps must have been a trying question. The dignity of the married woman depended somewhat upon the size of the cap she wore, and it was as necessary to convention that the crow-black locks of the [95] matron of twenty-five should be hidden, as that the scant locks of sixty should be decently shrouded.

Insertings of darned footing, alternating with bands of muslin, were largely used in the construction of gowns, and, in short, this style of needlework, while not as universal or absorbing as French embroidery, continued longer in vogue and perhaps amused or solaced some who had little skill or time for the more exacting methods of embroidery.

CHAPTER V   BERLIN WOOLWORK [96]

It surprises us in these latter days of demand for the best conditions in the prosecution of decorative work, that it should have lived at all through the days of existence in one-roomed log cabins of early settlers and the conflicting demands of pioneer life. It survived them all, and the little, fast-arriving Puritan children were taught their stitches as religiously as their commandments; and so American embroidery grew to be an art which has enriched the past and future of its executants.

After the two periods of French and Spanish needlework passed by, there appeared what was known as Berlin woolwork. Those who in earlier times were devoted to fine embroidery solaced their idleness with this new work—certainly a poor substitute for the beautiful embroidery of the preceding generation, but answering the purpose of traditional employment for the leisure class. This came into vogue and was rather extensively used for coverings of screens, chairs, sofas, footstools and the various specimens of household [97] furniture made by workmen who had served with Adam, Chippendale and Sheraton, and who had brought books of patterns with them to the prosperous, growing market of the New World. Berlin woolwork was a method of cross-stitch upon canvas in colored wools or silks—in fact, an extension of sampler methods into pictures and screens, or the more utilitarian chair and sofa covers. It was sometimes varied by using broadcloth or velvet as a foundation, the canvas threads being drawn out after the picture was complete. We occasionally find entire sets of beautiful old mahogany chairs, with cushions of cross-stitch embroidery, the subjects ranging over everything in the animal or vegetable world, so that one might sit in turn upon horses, bead-eyed and curled lap dogs, or wreaths of lilies and roses.

Occasionally, also, a glassed and framed picture of elaborate design and beautiful workmanship is seen, but as a rule it must be confessed that in America this method of embroidery, as an art, failed to achieve dignity. This was not in the least owing to the actual technique of the process, since beautiful tapestries have been accomplished, [98] taking canvas as a medium and foundation for a dexterous use of design and color.

The square blocks of the canvas stitch are no more objectionable in an art process than the block of enamel of which priceless mosaics are made, but one can easily see that if every design for mosaic work could be indefinitely reproduced and sold by the thousands, with numbered and colored blocks of glass, something — we hardly know what — would be lost in even the most exact reproductions.

Original design, however simple, is the expression of a thought, and passes directly from the mind of the originator to the material upon which it is expressed; but when the design becomes an article of commercial supply it loses in interest, and if the process of production is simple, requiring little thought and skill, the work also fails to call out in us the reverence we willingly accord to skillful and painstaking embroidery.

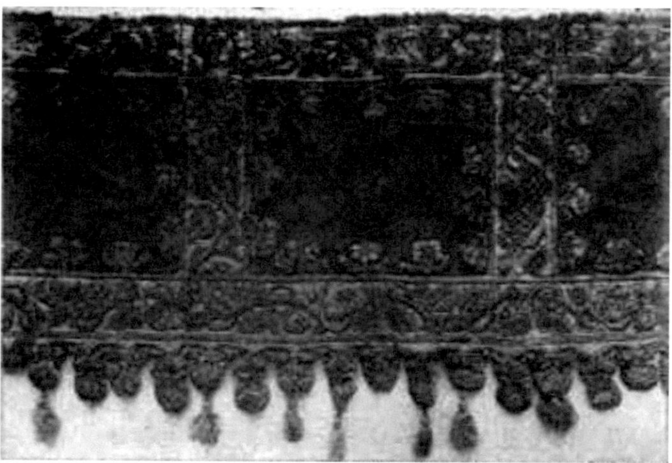

larger image

Courtesy of Brooklyn Museum

BED HANGING of polychrome cross-stitch appliquéd on blue woolen ground.

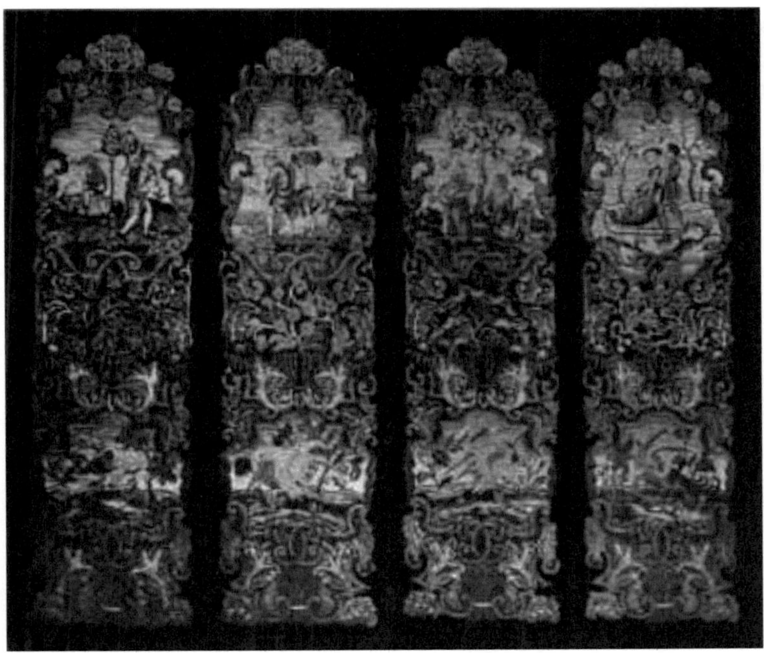

larger image

Courtesy of the Edgewater Tapestry Looms

NEEDLEPOINT SCREEN made in fine and coarse point. Single cross-stitch.

Yet we must acknowledge there are many examples of Berlin woolwork which possess the merits of beautiful color and exact and even workmanship. Some of them are done upon the finest of canvas with silks of exquisite shadings, and where figures are represented the faces are [99] worked with silk in "single stitch," which means one crossing of the canvas instead of two, as in ordinary cross-stitch. The latter was of course better suited for furniture coverings, both in strength and quality of surface, while the method of single stitch succeeded in presenting a smooth and well-shaded surface, sufficiently like a painted one to stand for a picture. Indeed, veritable pictures were produced in this method and were effective and interesting. In these specimens the faces and hands, while worked in the same cross-stitch, were varied by being done on a single crossing of the canvas with one stitch, while the costumes and accessories of the picture were done over the larger square of two threads of the canvas, with the double crossing of the stitch.

The faces were, in some cases, still further differentiated by being wrought in silk instead of wool threads.

The embroidered chair and sofa covers had quite the effect of tapestries, and were far better than a not uncommon variation of the same needlework, where the broadcloth or velvet background held the embroidery.

The designs were copied from patterns printed [100] in color upon cross-ruled paper, and consisted of bunches of flowers of various sorts, or pictures of dogs, and horses, and birds. A white lap dog worked upon a dark background was the favorite design for a footstool, and this small object tapered out the existence of decorative cross-stitch, until it grew to be in use only as a decoration for toilet slippers. The final end of this style of work was long deferred on account of the fact that a pair of cloth slippers, embroidered by the hands of some affectionate girl or doting woman, was a token which was not too unusual to carry inconvenient significance. It might mean much or little, much tenderness or affection, or a work of idleness tinctured with sentiment.

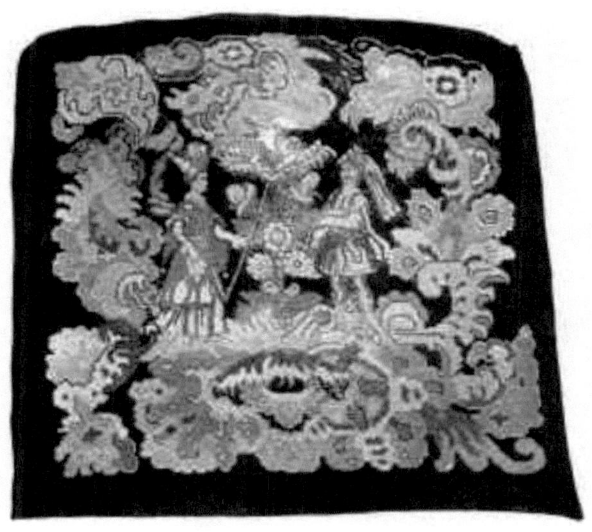

larger image

Courtesy of the Edgewater Tapestry Looms

HAND-WOVEN TAPESTRY of fine and coarse needlepoint.

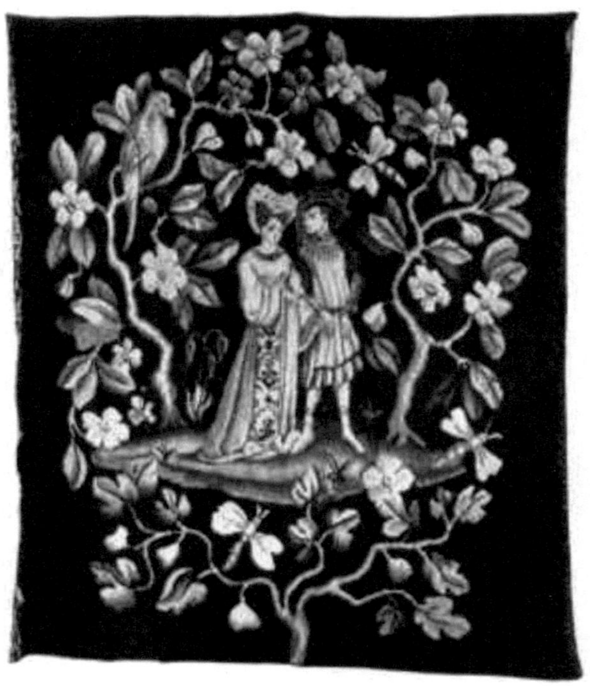

larger image

Courtesy of the Edgewater Tapestry Looms

TAPESTRY woven on a hand loom. The design worked in fine point and the background coarse point. A new effect in hand weave originated at the Edgewater Tapestry Looms.

The mechanical and commercial effect of this stitchery discouraged its use; its printed patterns and the regularity of its counted stitches giving neither provocation nor scope to originality of thought or design. This was not the fault of the stitch itself, since "cross-stitch" was the first form of needle decoration. It is, in fact, the A B C of all decorative stitchery, the method evolved by all primitive races except the American Indian. It followed, more or less closely, the [101] development of the art of weaving. When this had passed from the weaving together of osiers into mats or baskets, and had reached the stage of the weaving of hair and vegetable

114

fiber into cloth, the decoration of such cloth with independent colored fiber was the next step in the creation of values, and, naturally, the form of decorative stitches followed the lines of weaving. Simple as was its evolution, and its preliminary use, cross-stitch has a past which entitles it to reverence. With many races it has remained a habitual form of expression, and, as in Moorish and Algerian work, is carried to a refinement of beauty which would seem beyond so simple a method. It has given form to a lasting style of design, to geometrical borders, which have survived races and periods of history, and still remain an underlying part of the world of decorative linens.

It is interesting to note that it had no place in aboriginal embroidery, and marks its creation as following the art of weaving. It is a long step from this traditional past of its origin to the short past of the stitchery of America, where the little fingers of small Puritan maids followed the lines evolved by the generations of the earlier world.

CHAPTER VI REVIVAL OF EMBROIDERY, AND THE FOUNDING OF THE SOCIETY OF DECORATIVE ART [102]

When French needlework had had its day, and the evanescent life of Berlin woolwork had passed, for a period of half a century needlework ceased to flourish in America. Indeed, the art seemed to have died out root and branch, and only necessary and utilitarian needlework was practiced. It seems strange, after all the wonderful triumphs of the needle in earlier years, that for the succeeding half or three-quarters of a century needlework as an art should actually have ceased to be. It had died, branch and stem and root, vanished as if it had never been. During at least half a century we were a people without decorative needlework art in any form. The eyes and thoughts of women were turned in other directions.

Of course there is always a reason for a change in public taste, something in the development of the time leads and governs every trend of [103] popular thought. It may be the attraction of new inventions, or the perfection of new processes, or even, and this is not uncommon, the charm and fascination of some rare personality, whose ruling is absolute in its own immediate vicinity, and whose example spreads like circles in water far and far beyond the immediate personal influence. We cannot trace this apparent dearth of the art to one particular cause, we only know that in America the practice and study of music succeeded to its place in almost every household. The needle, that honored implement of woman, bade fair to be a thing almost of tradition, something which would be in time relegated to museums and collections, to be studied historically, as we study the implements of the Stone Age, and other prehistoric periods.

I remember an amusing story told by a Baltimore friend, not given to the manufacture of instances, that during those years of dearth soon after the Civil War she was visiting a lovely southern family who had lived through the days of privation. One day there arose a great cry and disturbance in the house, which turned out to be a quest for *the* needle, where was *the* needle. [104] Nobody could find it, although it could be proved that at a certain date it had been quilted into its accustomed place on the edge of the drawing-room curtain of the east window. Finally it was found on the wrong curtain, minus the point, and this disability gave rise to a discussion. Should it be taken to town, and have the point renewed by the watchmaker? This decision was discouraged by the daughter of the house, who related that the last time she had taken it for the same purpose, the watchmaker had said to her, "Miss Cassy, I have put a point on that needle three times, and I would seriously advise you to buy a new one."

It was only in America that the needle had ceased to be an active implement. In England it had never been so constantly or feverishly employed. For the second time in its long history, its work became purely personal. The same necessity which impressed itself upon the poor little mother of mankind, when she sought among the fig leaves for wherewithal to clothe herself, was upon the domestic woman, who sewed cloth into skirts instead of vegetable fiber into aprons.

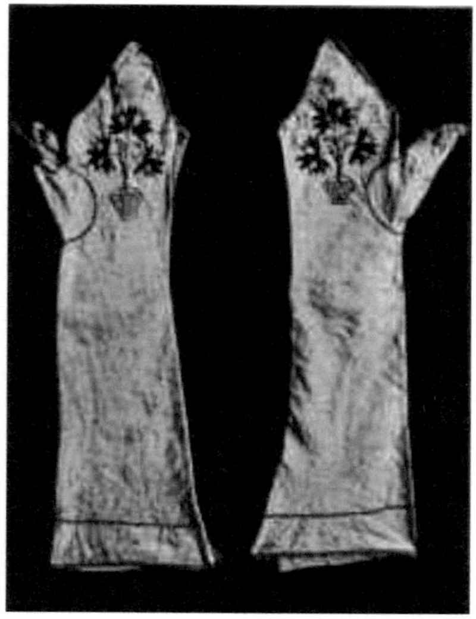

larger image

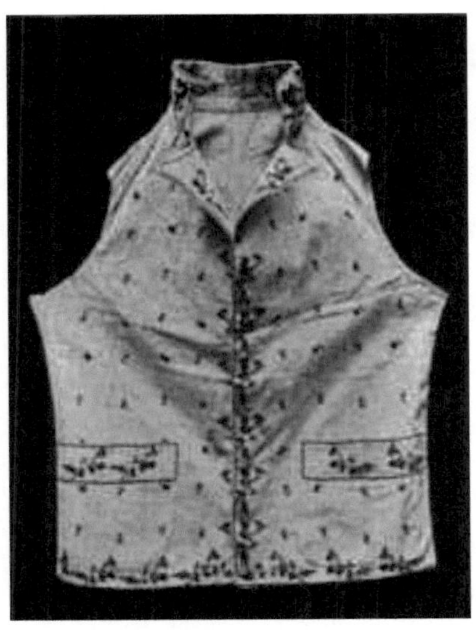

larger image

Courtesy Metropolitan Museum of Art

Left—EMBROIDERED MITS

Right—WHITE COTTON VEST embroidered in colors. Eighteenth-nineteenth century American.

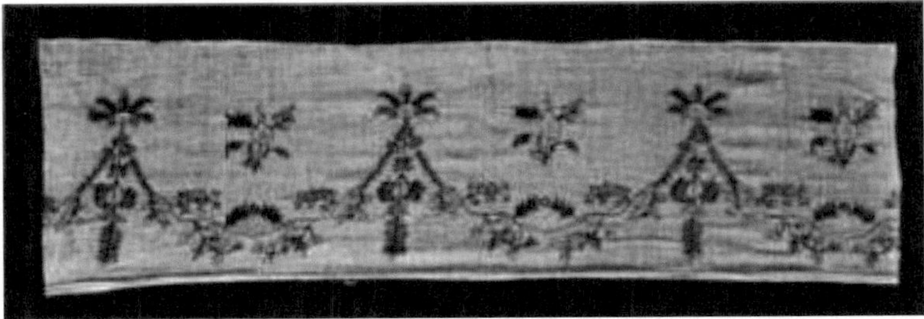

larger image

Courtesy Metropolitan Museum of Art

WHITE MULL embroidered in colors. Eighteenth-nineteenth century American.

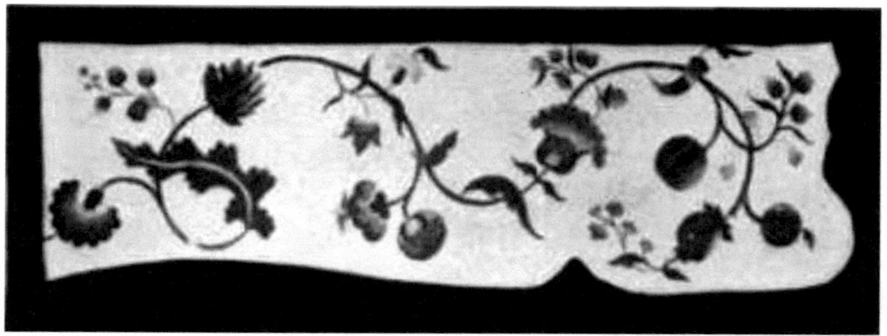

larger image

EMBROIDERED VALANCE, part of set and spread for high-post bedstead, 1788. Worked in crewels on India cotton, by Mrs. Gideon Granger, Canandaigua, New York.

It is curious to contrast the effect of this loss of [105] embroidery in the two countries, England and America. Doubtless there were other reasons than the lost popularity of needlework as an art, that in England it should have resulted in the life or death practice of necessary needlework, and in America, that the facile fingers of woman simply turned to the ivory keys of the piano for occupation. But the fact remains that starvation threatened the woman of one country, while in the other they were practicing scales. In England it was a period of stress and strain, of veritable "work for a living," the period of "The Song of the Shirt." Happily, in this blessed land, where hunger was unknown, we were not conscious of its terrors, and perhaps hardly knew why the "cambric needle" and the darning needle were the only ones in the market. Embroidery needles had "gone out." Then came the relief of the sewing machine, born in America, where it was scarcely needed, but speedily flying across the ocean to its life-saving work in England, where the tragedy of the poor seamstress was on the stage of life. Like many another form of relief, it was not entirely adequate to the situation. Its first effect was to create a need of remunerative [106] work. The sewing machine took upon itself the toil of the seamstress, but it left the seamstress idle and hungry. This was a new and even darker situation than the last, but Englishwomen came to the rescue with a resuscitated form of needlework and embroidery tiptoed upon the empty stage, new garments covering her ancient form, and was welcomed with universal acclaim.

120

Most cultivated and fortunate Englishwomen had a certain knowledge of art and were eager to put all of their uncoined effort at the service of that body of unhappy women, who, without money, had the culture which goes with the use and possession of money. These unfortunate sisters, who were rather malodorously called decayed gentlewomen, became eager and petted pupils of a new and popular organization called the South Kensington School. Its peculiar claims upon English society gave it from the first the help of the most advanced and intelligent artistic assistance. The result of this was not only a resuscitation of old methods of embroidery, but the great gain to the school, or society, of design and criticism of such men as Burne-Jones, Walter Crane, and William Morris. [107]

It was with this vogue that it appeared in America, and attracted the attention of those who were afterward to be interested in the formation of a society which was founded for almost identical purposes. Not indeed to prevent starvation of body, but to comfort the souls of women who pined for independence, who did not care to indulge in luxuries which fathers and brothers and husbands found it hard to supply. So, from what was perhaps a social and mental, rather than a physical, want, grew the great remedy of a resuscitation of one of the valuable arts of the world, a woman's art, hers by right of inheritance as well as peculiar fitness.

With true business enterprise, the new English Society prepared an important exhibit for our memorial fair, the Centennial, held in Philadelphia to mark the one-hundredth anniversary of national independence. This exhibit of Kensington Embroidery all unwittingly sowed the seed not only of great results, but in decorative art worked in many other directions. The exhibits of art needlework from the New Kensington School of Art in London, their beauty, novelty and easy adaptiveness, exactly fitted it to experiment by all [108] the dreaming forces of the American woman. They were good needlewomen by inheritance and sensitive to art influences by nature, and the initiative capacity which belongs to power and feeling enabled them at once to seize upon this mode of expression and make it their own. It was the means of inaugurating another era of true decorative needlework, perfectly adapted to the capacity of all women, and destined to be developed on lines peculiarly national in character. The effect of this exhibit was not exactly what was expected in the sale of its works, and long afterward, when discussing this apparent failure, in the face of an immediate adoption in America of the Society's methods and productions, I explained it to myself and an English friend, by the national difference in the race feeling for art, and especially for color.

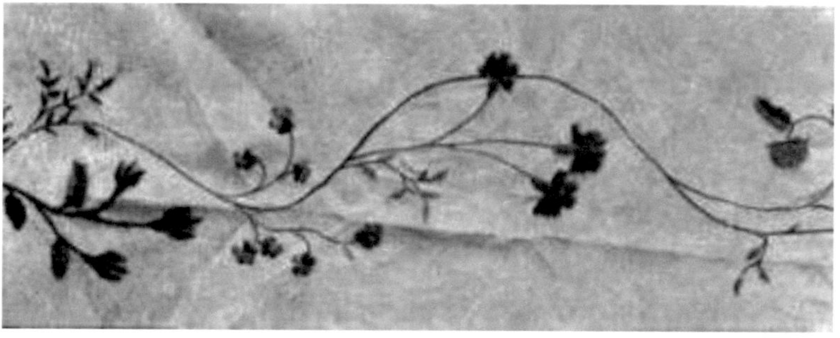

larger image

Courtesy of Brooklyn Museum

DETAIL of linen coverlet worked in colored wool.

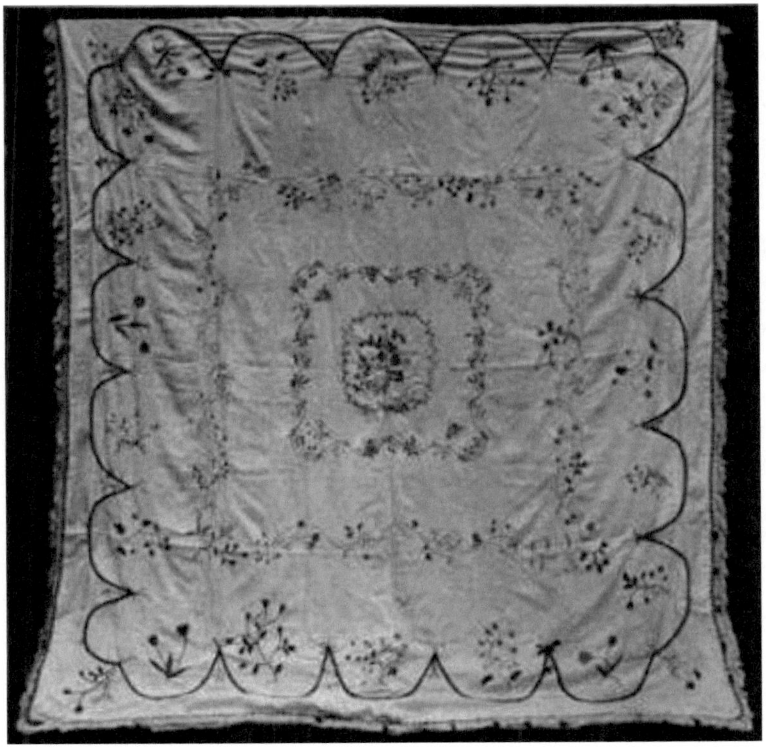

larger image

Courtesy of Brooklyn Museum

LINEN COVERLET embroidered in Kensington stitch with colored wool.

It seems to me, after the observation and intimacy of years with the growing art of decoration in this country, that the color gift is a race gift with us. English art-work is nearly always characterized by subdued and modified harmony, while that of America has vivid and striking notes which play upon a higher key, [109] and still melt as softly into each other as the perfect modulations of the best English art. I was very conscious of this during the year of my directorship of the Woman's Building and exhibits in the World's Columbian Fair at Chicago, that place of wonderful comparisons of the art-work of the world. I could nearly always recognize work of American origin by its singing color-quality, as different from the sharp semibarbaric notes of Oriental art as from the minor cadences of English decorative work. But to return to the effect of the English exhibit at the Philadelphia Centennial: it was followed by the immediate formation of the Society of Decorative Art in New York City, which became the parent of like societies in every considerable city or town in the United States. By its good fortune in having a president who belonged by right of birth, and certainly of ability and achievement, to the best of New York society, the movement enlisted the sympathy and interest of the influential class of New York women, while there was waiting in the shadow a troop of able women who were shut out from the costly gayeties of society by comparative poverty, but connected [110] with it by friendships and associations, often, indeed, by ties of blood.

Embroidery became once more the most facile and successful of pursuits. Graduates from the Kensington School were employed as teachers in nearly all of the different societies, and in this way every city became the center of this new-old form of embroidery, for what is called "Kensington Embroidery" is in fact a far-away repetition of old triumphs of the British needle. I use the word "British" advisedly, for it was when England was known as Britain among the nations that her embroidery was a thing of almost priceless value. In modern English embroidery, the days of Queen Anne have been the limit of backward imitation; and, in fact, ancient English embroidery was a process of long and assiduous labor, as well as of knowledge and inspiration. Our hurried modern conditions would not encourage the repetition of the hand-breadth pictures in embroidery of the earliest specimens, where countless numbers of stitches were lavished upon a single production. The embroidered picture of The Garden of Eden described in chapter four is a specimen of the minute representation. These specimens are, to [111] the art of needlework, what the Dutch school of painting is to the great mural canvases of the present day.

The development of the nineteenth century in America was only at first an exact reflection of English methods. The first thing which marked the influence of national character and taste was, that English models and designs almost immediately disappeared, only a few such, consisting of those which had been given to the art by masters of design like Morris and Marcus Ward, were retained, and American needlewomen boldly took to the representation of vivid and graceful groups of natural flowers, following the lead of Moravian practice and of flower painting, rather than that of decorative design.

As a natural result, crewels were soon discarded in favor of silks, and natural extravagance, or national influence, led to the use of costly materials instead of the linens of English choice and preference. So the old flower embroidery of Bethlehem had a second birth. American girl art-students soon found their opportunity in the creation of applied design, and before embroidery had ceased to be a matter of representation of [112] flowers in colored silks, the flowers grew into restrained and appropriate borders, or proper and correct space decoration, and the day of women designers for manufacturers had come.

The circulars of the first Society of Decorative Art were not only comprehensive, but were ambitious. Its objects were set forth as follows:

1. To encourage profitable industries among women who possess artistic talent, and to furnish a standard of excellence and a market for their work.

2. To accumulate and distribute information concerning the various art industries which have been found remunerative in other countries, and to form classes in Art Needlework.

3. To establish rooms for the exhibition and sale of Sculptures, Paintings, Wood Carvings, Paintings upon Slate, Porcelain and Pottery, Lacework, Art and Ecclesiastical Needlework, Tapestries and Hangings, and, in short, decorative work of any description, done by women, and of sufficient excellence to meet the recently stimulated demand for such work.

4. To form Auxiliary Committees in other cities and towns of the United States, which committees shall receive and pronounce upon work produced in, or in the vicinity of, such places, and which, if approved by them, may be consigned to the salesrooms in New York.

5. To make connections with potteries, by which desirable forms for decoration, or original designs for special [113] orders, may be procured, and with manufacturers and importers of the various materials used in art work, by which artists may profit.

6. To endeavor to obtain orders from dealers in China, Cabinet Work, or articles belonging to Household Art throughout the United States.

7. To induce each worker thoroughly to master the details of one variety of decoration, and endeavor to make for her work a reputation of commercial value.

The Society meets an actual want in the community by furnishing a place where orders can be given directly to the artist for any kind of art or decorative work on exhibition.

It is believed that, by the encouragement of this Society, the large amount of work done by those who do not make it a profession will be brought to the notice of buyers outside a limited circle of friends. The aggregate of this work is large, and when directed into remunerative channels will prove a very important department of industry.

The necessary expenses of the Society for the first, and possibly the second, year will be defrayed by a membership fee of Five Dollars, as well as by donations; but after that time it is expected that all expenses will be met by commissions upon the sale of articles consigned to it.

The contributions of all women artists of acknowledged ability are earnestly requested. By their co-operation it is intended that a high standard of excellence shall be established in what is offered to the public, and, by seeing truly artistic decorative work, it is hoped many women [114] who have found the painting of pictures unremunerative may turn their efforts in more practical directions.

All work approved by the Committee of Examination will be attractively exhibited without expense to the artist, but in case of sale a commission of 10 per cent will be charged upon the price received.

There was good teaching from the first, but very independent judgment, and it was not long before the more liberal and less chastened American mind followed national impulses. Why, said the practical American, shall we spend time and effort in doing things which are not adequate in final effect to the labor and cost we bestow upon them, and which do not really accord with costly surroundings, and, in addition to these detriments, can and probably will be eaten by moths when all is done? The result of this interrogative reasoning was an immediate resort to satins and silks and flosses, wherewith larger and more important things than tidies were created—lambrequins, hangings, bedspreads, screens, and many other furnishings, all wrought in exquisite flosses, and more or less beautiful in color.

The institution of this Society of Decorative Art was in every respect a timely and popular [115] movement. It followed the example of the English Society in making needlework the chief object of instruction. Our artists became interested in the matter of design, as the English artists had been, and under their influence the scope of embroidery was much enlarged. I remember the first contribution which indicated original talent was a piece of needlework by Mrs. W. S. Hoyt of Pelham, which was peculiarly ingenious, making a curious link between the cross-stitch tapestries of the German school and the woven tapestries of France. This needlework was done upon a fabric which imitated the corded texture of tapestries, and was stamped in a design which carried the color and idea of a tapestry background. Upon this surface Mrs. Hoyt had drawn a group of figures in mediæval costumes, afterward working them in single cross-stitch over the ribs produced by the filling threads of the fabric. The figures and costumes were done in faded tints which harmonized with the background, the stitches keeping the general effect of surface in the fabric. It will be seen that the result was extremely like that of a tapestry of the fifteenth century. This was [116] followed by an exhibit of various landscape pictures of Mrs. Holmes of Boston, a daughter-in-law of the poet and writer. Mrs. Holmes had chosen silks and bits of weavings for her medium, using them as a painter uses colors upon his palette. A stretch of pale blue silk, with outlined hills lying against it, made for her a sky and background, while a middle distance of flossy white stitches, advancing into well-defined daisies, brought the foreground to one's very feet. Flower-laden apple branches against the sky were lightly sketched in embroidery stitches, like the daisies. It was a delicious bit of color and so well managed as to be as efficient a wall decoration as a water color picture.

In what may be called pictorial art in textiles Mrs. Holmes was not alone, although her work probably incited to the same sort of experiment. Miss Weld of Boston sent a picture made up in the same way, of a background of material which lent itself to the representation of a field of swampy ground where the spotted leaves of the adder's tongue, the yellow water-lily, with its compact balls, and the flaming cardinal flower are growing, while swamp grasses are nodding [117] above. This was as good in its way as any sketch of them could be, and affected one with the *sentiment* of the scene, as it is the mission of art to do. Miss Weld, Miss Carolina Townshend of Albany, Mrs. William Hoyt of Pelham and Mrs. Dewey of New York, each contributed very largely to the formation of characteristic and progressive needlework art in America. There were other individuals whose work was inciting many, who have also, perhaps unknown to themselves, helped in this progress. Indeed, I remember many pieces of embroidery, loaned for the Bartholdi Exhibition of 1883, which would have done credit to any period of the art, and each piece undoubtedly had its influence.

The work of schools or societies had been much less marked by original development. During the ten years of their existence the four largest societies, those of New York, Boston, Philadelphia and Chicago, have been under the direction of English teachers, and have followed more or less closely the excellencies of the English School. Even in Boston, where, owing to the decided cultivation of art and the early introduction of drawing in the public schools, one would have [118] looked for a rather characteristic development, English designs and English methods have been somewhat closely followed.

In attempting to account for this fact one must remember that it is against the nature of associated authority to follow individual or original suggestions. There must be a broad and well-trodden path for committees to walk together in, and the track of the Kensington School is broad and authoritative enough for such following. The example and incitement of the various societies were the seed of much good and progressive art in America. In saying this I do not by any means confine the credit of the growth or development of needlework to this society alone, for there have been other influences at work. What I mean to say is this, that the other kindred societies, like the Woman's Exchange, the Needlework Societies, the Household Art Societies, and the Blue-and-White Industries started from this one root, and are as much indebted to the original society as things must always be to the central thought which inspired them. Compared with English work of the same period, they were distinguished by a certain spontaneity of motive [119] and a luxuriance of effect, which has made these specimens more valuable to present possessors, and will make them far more precious as heirlooms. This sudden efflorescence of the art was, however, almost in the hands of amateurs, except for the occasional effort by some of the advanced contributors of the New York and Boston societies.

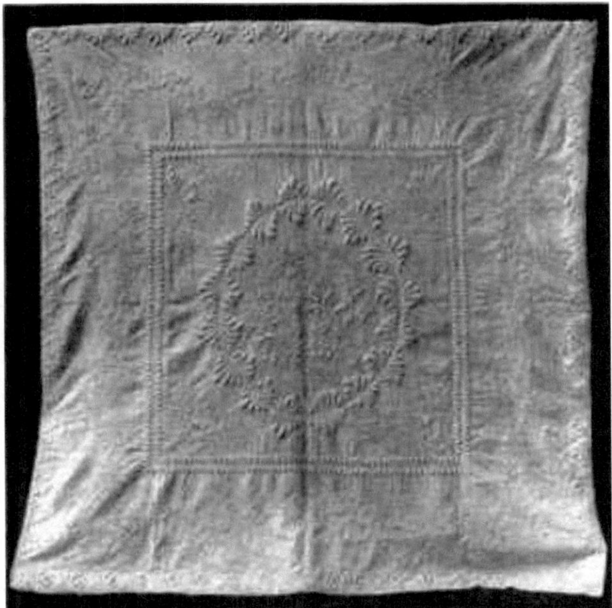

larger image

Courtesy of Brooklyn Museum

QUILTED COVERLET worked entirely by hand.

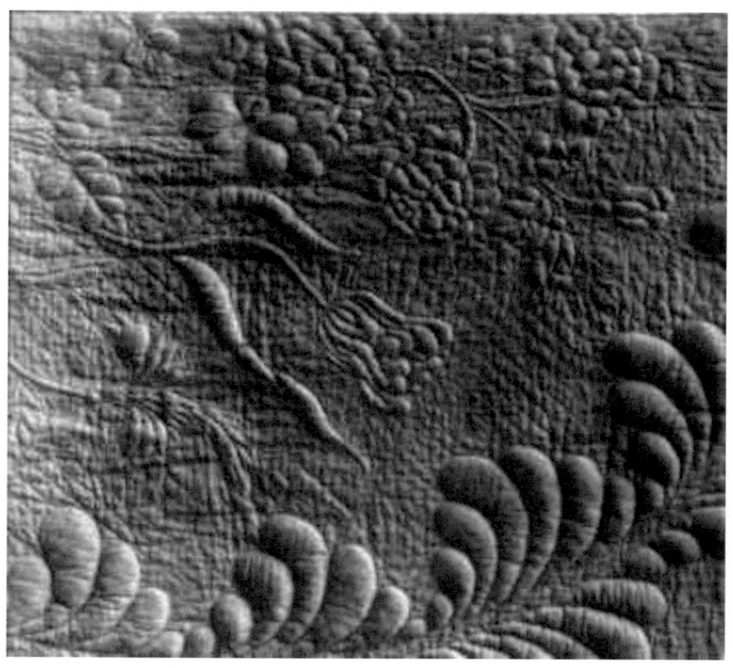

larger image

Courtesy of Brooklyn Museum

DETAIL of above coverlet.

The commercial development of embroidery in this country has been in the direction of embroidery upon linen, and in this line each and every society of decorative art has been a center of valuable teaching. At the Columbian Exposition, to which all prominent societies contributed, the perfection of design, color and method, the general level of excellence, was on the highest possible plane. In its line nothing could be better, and it was encouraging to see that it was *not* amateur work, *not* a thing to be taken up and laid down according to moods and circumstances, but an educated profession or occupation for women, the acquirement of a knowledge which might develop indefinitely.

Of course the trend of the decorative needlework was almost entirely in the direction of stitchery pure and simple, devoted to table

[120] linen and luxurious household uses, and this grew to a point of absolute perfection. Table-centers and doilies embroidered in colors on pure white linen reached a point of beauty which was amazing. When I saw, at the World's Columbian Exposition, the napery of the world, wrought by all races of women, I was delighted to see that the line of linen embroidery which was the direction of the common effort did not in the least surpass the work sent by the Decorative Art societies of most of our American cities.

The Society of Decorative Art, has proved itself a means for the accomplishment of the two ends for which it was founded — namely, the fostering and incitement of good taste in needlework and artistic production, and the encouragement of talent in women, as well as providing a means of remunerative employment for their gifts in this direction.

While the success of this Society was a source of great satisfaction to me, I had in my mind larger ambitions, which, by its very philanthropic purposes, could not be satisfied, ambitions toward a truly great American effort in a lasting direction.

I therefore allied myself with a newly formed group of men, all well-known in their own lines of art, Louis Tiffany, famed for his Stained Glass, Mr. Coleman for color decoration and the use of textiles, and Mr. De Forest for carved and ornamental woodwork. My interests lay in the direction and execution of embroideries. I can speak authoritatively as to the effect upon it of the other arts, and I can hardly imagine better [122] conditions for its development. The kindred arts of weaving and embroidery were carried on with those of stained glass, mural painting, illustration, and the other expressions of art peculiar to the different members. The association of different forms of art stimulated and developed and was the means of producing very important examples both in embroidery, needle-woven tapestries and loom weaving.

As I was the woman member of this association of artists, it rested with me to adapt the feminine art, which was a part of its activities, to the requirements of the association. This was no small task. It meant the fitting of any and every textile used in the furnishing of a house to its use and place, whether it might be curtains, portieres, or wall coverings. I drew designs which would give my draperies a framing which carried out the woodwork, and served as backgrounds for the desired wreaths and garlands of embroidered flowers. I learned many valuable lessons of adaptation for the beautiful embroideries we produced. The net holding roses was a triumph of picturesque stitchery, and most acceptable as placed in the house of the man whose fortunes [123] depended upon fish, and many another of like character.

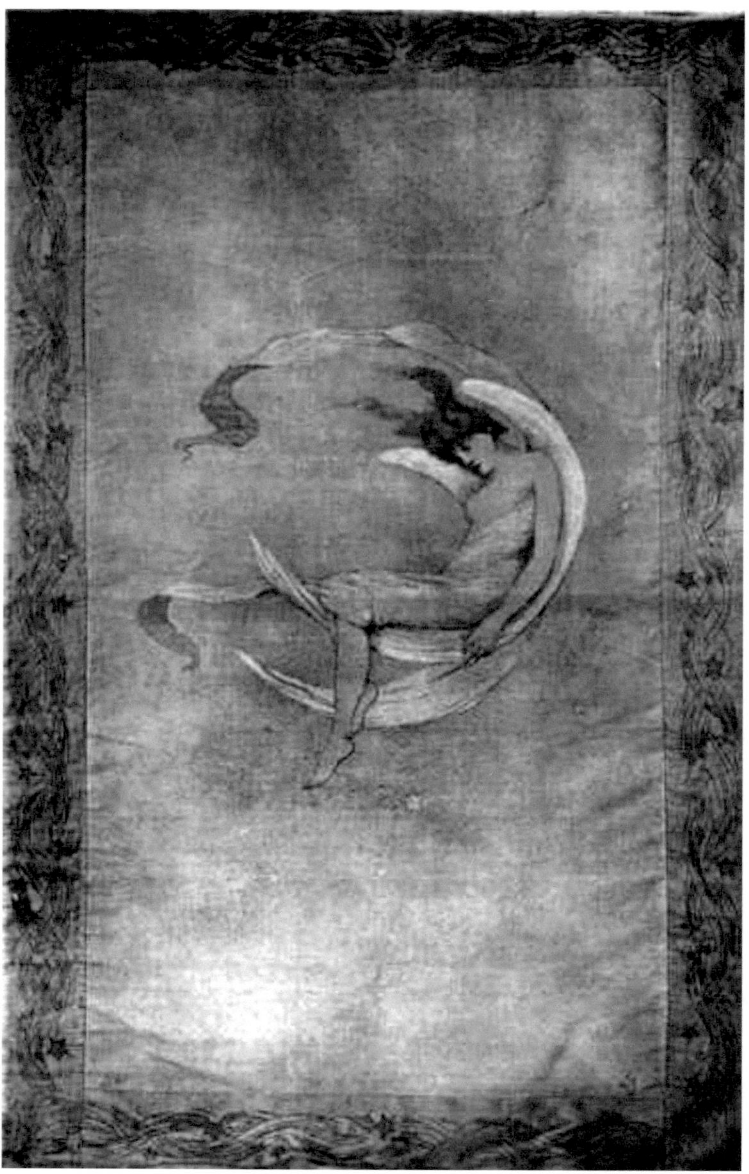

larger image

THE WINGED MOON

Designed by Dora Wheeler and executed in needle-woven tapestry by The Associated Artists, 1883.

Then one day appeared Mrs. Langtry in her then radiance of beauty, insisting upon a conference with me upon the production of a set of bed-hangings which were intended for the astonishment of the London world and to overshadow all the modest and schooled productions of the Kensington, when she herself should be the proud exhibitor. She looked at all the beautiful things we had done and were doing, and admired and approved, but still she wanted "something different, something unusual." I suggested a canopy of our strong, gauze-like, creamy silk bolting-cloth, the tissue used in flour mills for sifting the superfine flour. I explained that the canopy could be crosses on the under side with loops of full-blown, sunset-colored roses, and the hanging border heaped with them. That there might be a coverlet of bolting-cloth lined with the delicatest shade of rose-pink satin, sprinkled plentifully with rose petals fallen from the wreaths above. This idea satisfied the pretty lady, who seemed to find great pleasure in the range of our exhibits, our designs and our workrooms, and when [124] her order was completed, she was triumphantly satisfied with its beauty and unusualness. The scattered petals were true portraits done from nature, and looked as though they could be shaken off at any minute. I came to see much of this beautiful specimen of womanhood, who played her part in the eyes of the world; and of things of more lasting importance than her somewhat ephemeral career, I should be tempted to tell amusing conclusions. She was an Oriental butterfly, which flitted along our sober, serious by-path of business and labor, looking for honey of any sort to be gathered on its sober track.

When Mr. Tiffany came to me with an order for the drop-curtain of a theater, I did not trouble myself about a scheme for it, knowing that it had probably taken exact and interesting form in his own mind. It was a beautiful lesson to me, this largeness of purpose in needlework. The design for this curtain turned out to be a very realistic view of a vista in the woods, which gave opportunity for wonderful studies of color, from clear sun-lit foregrounds to tangles of misty green, melting into blue perspectives of distance. It was really a daring experiment in methods of [125] appliqué, for no stitchery pure and simple was in place in the wide reaches of the picture. So we went on painting a woods interior in materials of all sorts, from tenuous crêpes to solid velvets and plushes. It was one of Mrs. Holmes' silk pictures on a large scale, and was perhaps more than reasonably successful. I remember the great delight in marking the difference between oak and birch trees and fitting each with its appropriate effect of color and texture of leaf; and the building of a tall gray-green yucca, with its thick satin leaves and tall white pyramidal groups of velvet blossoms, standing in the very foreground, was as exciting as if it were standing posed for its portrait, and being painted in oils.

The variety of our work was a good influence for progress. We were constantly reaching out to fill the various demands, and, beyond them, to materialize our ideals. As far as art was concerned in our work, what we tried to do was not to repeat the triumphs of past needlework, but to see how far the best which had been done was applicable to the present.

If tapestries had been the highest mark of the past, to see whether and how their use could be [126] fitted to the circumstances of today, and, if we found a fit place for them in modern decoration, to see that their production took account of the methods and materials which belonged to present periods, and adapted the production to modern demands.

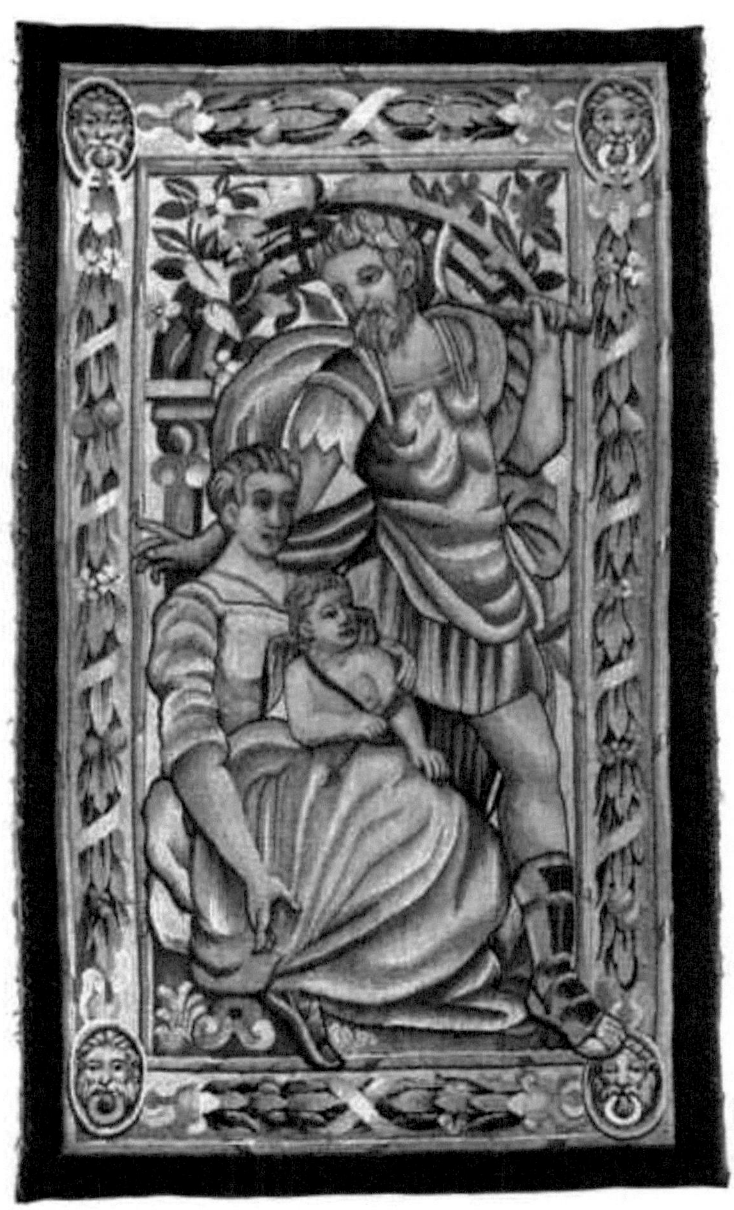

larger image

Courtesy of the Edgewater Tapestry Looms

SEVENTEENTH CENTURY DESIGN TAPESTRY PANEL

We soon came to the ideal of tapestries which loomed above and beyond us and had been reached by every nation in turn which had applied art to textiles, but in all except very early work the accomplishment had been more of the loom than of hand work. My dream was of American Tapestries, made by embroidery alone, carrying personal thought into method. We decided that there was no reason for the limitation of the beautiful art of needlework to personal use, or even to its numerous domestic purposes. This most intimate of the arts of decoration has been in the form of wall hangings for the bare wall spaces of architecture from the time when dwellings passed their first limited use of protection and defense. After this first use of houses came the instinct and longing for beauty, and the feeling which prompts us in these wider days of achievement to cover our wall spaces with [127] pictures, moved our far-off forefathers and mothers to offer their skill in spinning, and weaving, and picturing with the needle hangings to cover the bareness of the home. This impulse grew with the centuries, until tapestries were a natural art expression of different races of men, so that we have Italian, Spanish, French, Dutch and English tapestries, each with national tastes and characteristics of production. As time went on, inevitable machinery undertook the task of making wall hangings, with the whole-hearted help of all who had given their lives to art, and tapestries had become a part of the riches of the world. When the greater part of the world's wealth was in the possession of Popes and Princes, it was usual to expend a goodly portion of it in works of art. Pictures and tapestries and exquisitely wrought metal work, weavings and embroideries, made priceless by costly materials and the thoughts and labor of artists, were reckoned not as a sign of wealth but as actual wealth. They were really riches, as much as stocks and bonds are riches today. Such things were accumulated as anxiously and persistently as one accumulates land or houses, or railroad bonds or stocks, and [128] the buyer was not poorer; but in fact he was richer for money expended in this fashion. This every-day financial fact lay underneath and supported the beautiful pageant of the fifteenth and sixteenth centuries, gilding them with a radiance which has attracted the admiration and excited the wonder of all succeeding years.

That flower and culmination of labor which we call art was the capital of those early centuries, and took the place of the Bank, the Bourse, and the Exchange which later financial ideas have created.

It is in a great measure to this fact, as well as to the intense love for, and appreciation of, art which distinguished this period, that we owe the wonderful treasures which have enriched the later world. They belong no longer to princes and prelates, but to governments and museums, and are object lessons to the student and the artisan, and an inheritance for both rich and poor of all mankind.

Except in the light of these treasures of art, it would be difficult to understand how far-reaching and comprehensive was the greed of beauty which possessed and distinguished the [129] centers of tapestry production. The museums of the world are made up of what remains of them. The pictures and tapestries, the weavings and embroideries, the carvings and metal work which the world is studying, belonged to the daily life of those past centuries. The stamp of thought and the seal of art were set upon the simplest conveniences of life. The very keys of the locks and hinges of the doors were designed, not by mere workers in metal, but by sculptors and artists who were pre-eminent for genius. It was in the spirit of this period that Benvenuto Cellini modeled saltcellars as well as statues, and his compeers designed carvings and gildings for state carriages, and painted pictures upon the panels. Painters of divine pictures designed cartoons and borders for tapestries, and wreaths and garlands for ceiling pilasters.

Among the names of painters who designed cartoons for tapestries, we find those of Leonardo da Vinci, Raphael, Titian, Guido and Giulio Romano, Albert Dürer, Rubens and Van Dyck. Indeed, there is hardly a great name among the painters of the sixteenth and seventeenth centuries which has not contributed to the value of the [130] tapestries dating from those times. Among them all none have a greater share of glory than the series known as "The Acts of the Apostles," designed by Raphael for Pope Leo X, in the year 1515.

The history of these cartoons is full of interest. After the weaving of the first set of these tapestries, which was hung in the Sistine Chapel and regarded as among the greatest treasures of the world, the cartoons remained for more than a hundred years in the manufactory at Brussels. During this period one or more sets must have been woven from them, but in 1630 seven were transferred to the Mortlake Tapestry works near London, having been purchased by Charles I, who was advised of their existence by Rubens. The Mortlake tapestry had been established by James I, who was greatly aided by the interest of the then Prince of Wales, and the Duke of Buckingham. It is charming to think of "Baby Charles" and "Steenie" busying themselves with the encouragement of art in the way of the production of tapestry pictures, and after the accession of the Prince, to follow the progress of this taste in the purchase of the famous cartoons, and the employment of no less a genius than [131] Van Dyck in the composition of new and more elaborate borders for them. It was probably during the reign of Charles that these glorious compositions went into use as illustrations of Biblical text, for we find "Paul preaching at Athens," "Peter and Paul at the Beautiful Gate of the Temple," and "The Miraculous Draught of Fishes" figuring as full-page frontispieces to many old copies of King James' Bible. After the tragic close of the reign of King Charles, the treasures of tapestries he had accumulated were dispersed and sold by order of Cromwell; but the cartoons remained the property of the nation and, though lost to sight for another hundred years or so, finally reappeared from their obscurity, at Hampton Court, and in these later years, at the Kensington Museum, have again taken their place as one of the most valuable lessons of earlier centuries. It was probably the story of these cartoons which inspired the determination which had taken possession of us, to do a real tapestry, something greatly worthy of accomplishment.

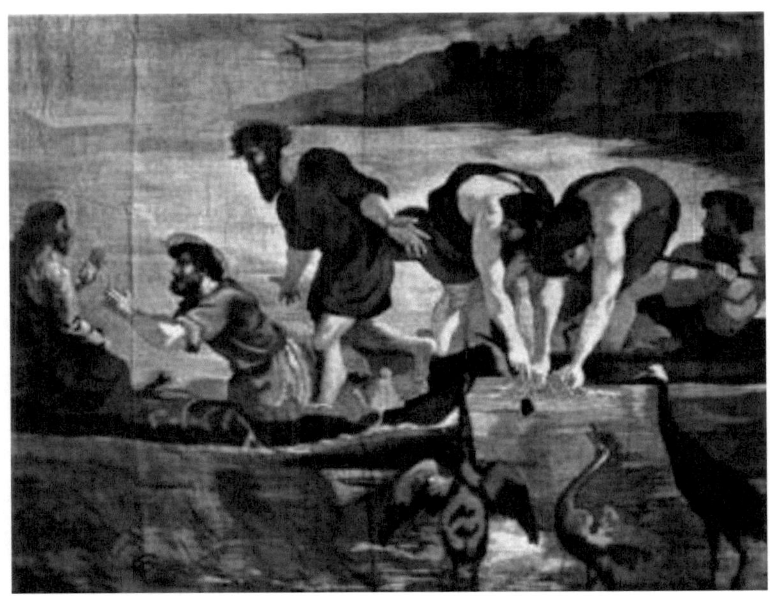

larger image

THE MIRACULOUS DRAUGHT OF FISHES

Arranged (from photographs made in London of the original cartoon by Raphael, in the Kensington Museum) by Candace Wheeler and executed in needle-woven tapestry by the Associated Artists.

When we came to the decision to create tapestries, the actual substance of them, as well as [132] the art, was a thing to be considered. The wool fiber upon which they were usually based was a prey to many enemies. Dust may corrupt and moths utterly destroy fiber of wool, but dust does not accumulate on threads of silk, neither are they quite acceptable to the appetite of moths. Therefore, we reasoned, if we did work which was worthy of comparative immortality, it must be done with comparatively imperishable material. Fiber of flax and fiber of silk shared this advantage, and the silk was tenacious of color, which was not the case with flax; therefore we chose silk and went bravely to our task of creating American tapestries.

Having decided upon our material, we consulted with our friendly and interested manufacturers, and finally ordered a broad, heavily marked, loosely woven fabric which would hold our precious stitches safely and show them to advantage. The woof of the canvas upon which we were to experiment was also of silk, not fine and twisted like the warp, but soft and full enough to hold silk stitchery. In this way the face of the canvas, or ground, could be quite covered by a full thread of embroidery silk passed [133] under the slender warp and actually sewn into the woof.

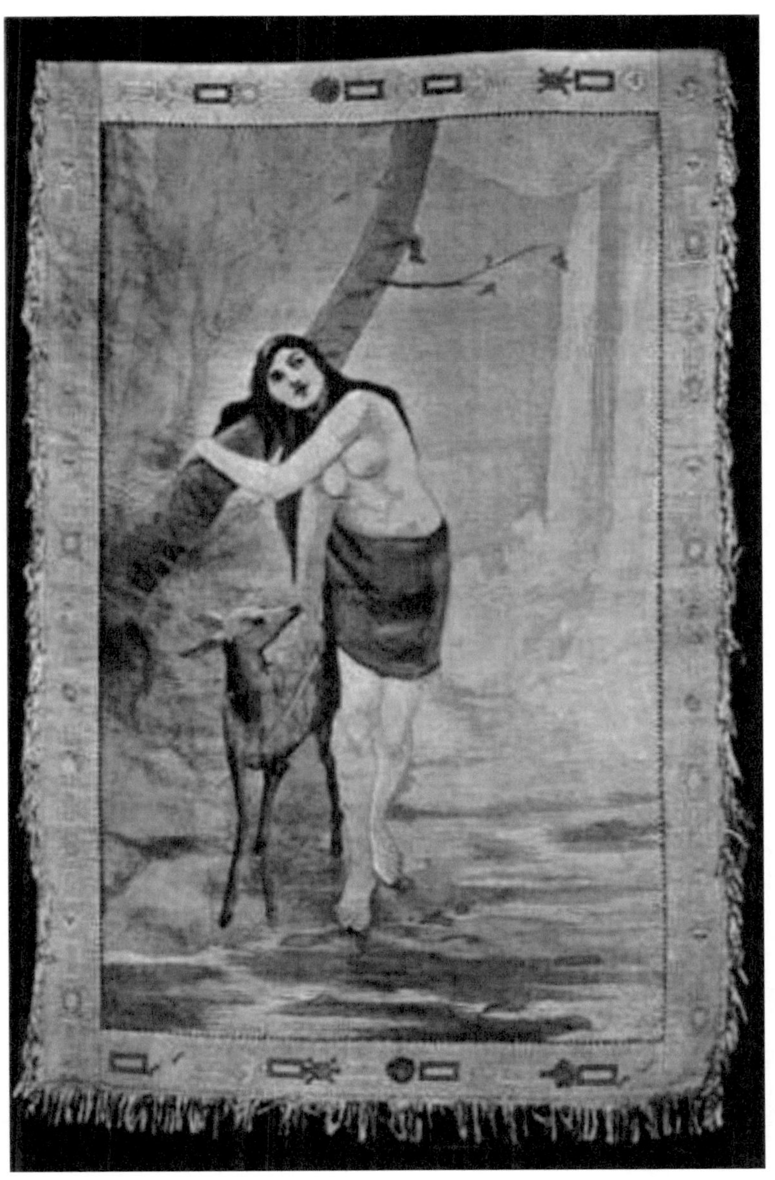

larger image

MINNEHAHA LISTENING TO THE WATERFALL

Drawn by Dora Wheeler and executed in needle-woven tapestry by The Associated Artists, 1884.

Being thus fully equipped for the production of real tapestries, well adapted to the processes of what I called "needle weaving," since the needle was really used as a shuttle to carry threads over and under the already fixed warp, the next decision rested upon the subject of this new application of the art and the knowledge we had gained by study and practice and love of textile art. With a courage which we now wonder at, we selected perhaps the most difficult, as it certainly is the most beautiful, of surviving tapestries, "The Miraculous Draught of Fishes," the cartoon of which, designed by Raphael, is at present to be seen and studied at the Kensington Museum in London. The decision to copy this was perhaps influenced by the fact that it was the only original cartoon of which I had knowledge, and my summer holiday in London was spent in its study, and schemes for its exact reproduction. As it was spread upon a wall in museum fashion, a drawing could not be actually verified by measurements, but an expedient came to me which proved to be satisfactory. I had [134] two photographs, as large as possible, made from the cartoon, and one of them, being very faintly printed, copied exactly in color; the other was ruled and cut into squares, and was again photographed and enlarged to a size which would bring them, when joined, to the same measurements as the original cartoon. These, very carefully put together, made a working drawing for my tapestry copy, and the lighter photograph, which had been most carefully water-colored, gave the color guide for the copy.

It was interesting to find the perforations along the lines of the composition still showing in the photographed cartoon, and we made use of them by going over them with pin pricks, fastening the cartoon over the sheet of silk canvas woven for the background, so that there was no possibility of shifting. Prepared powder was sifted through the lines of perforation and fixed by the application of heat, and we then had the entire composition exactly outlined upon the ground. After that the work of superimposing color and shading by needle weaving was a labor of love and diligent fingers during

144

many months. Every inch of stitchery was carefully criticized [135] and constantly compared with the colored copy, and at last it was a finished tapestry and was hung in a north light on one of the great spaces of the studio, where it was an object of expert examination and general admiration.

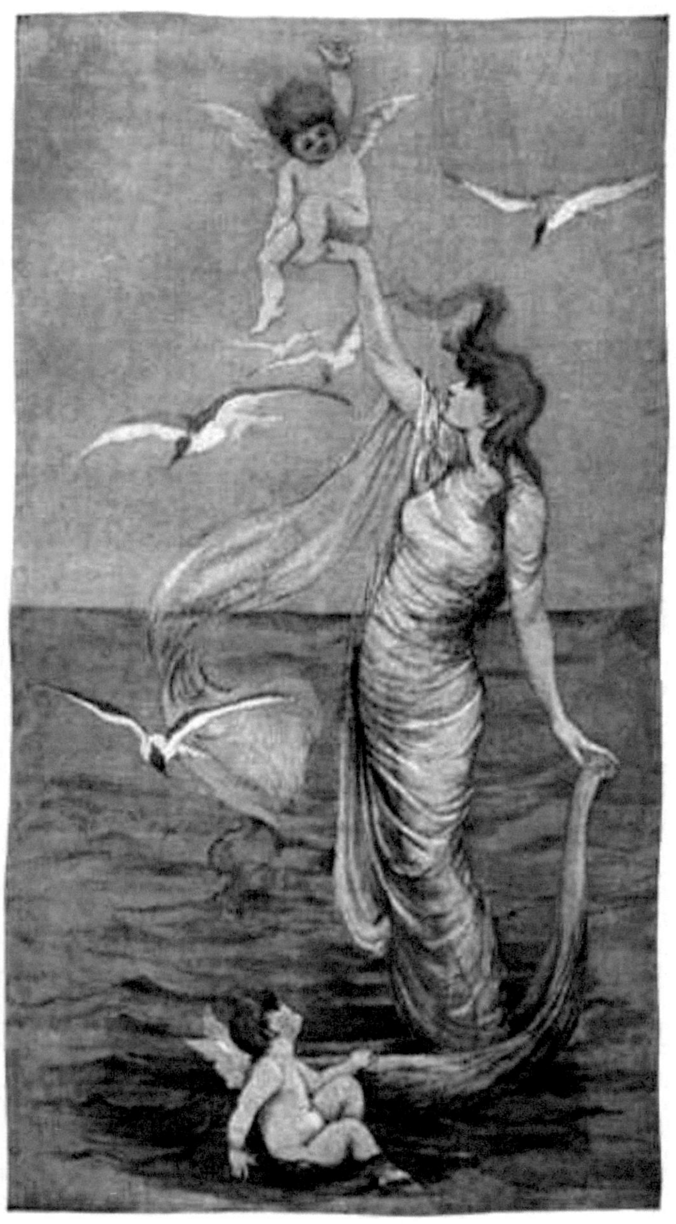

larger image

APHRODITE

Designed by Dora Wheeler for needle-woven tapestry worked by The Associated Artists, 1883.

It is by far the most important work accomplished by needle weaving which has ever been made in America, and is as veritable a copy of the original as if it were painted with brush and pigment, instead of being woven with threads of silk. The low lights of the evening sky, the reflections of the boats, and the stooping figures of the fishermen, the perspective of the distant shore, and the wonderful grouping in the foreground, keep their charm in the tapestry as they do in the picture. Even the mystery of the twilight is rendered, with the subtle effect we feel, but can scarcely define, in the original drawing.

It has been a curiously direct process from the hand of the great master, to this new reproduction, although it stands so far from his time and life. His very thought was painted by his very hand upon the paper of the cartoon, and this painted thought has been photographed upon [136] another paper which has served as a guide to the copy.

It makes us sharers in the art riches of Raphael's own time, to see a new embodiment of his thought appearing as a part of the nineteenth century's accomplishments and possessions.

After this achievement we naturally began to look for appropriate use for the small tapestries, but here came our stumbling block. The breed of princes, who had been the former patrons of such works of art, were all asleep in their graves, and knew not America, or its ambitions, and our native breed was not an hereditary one, building galleries in palaces, and collecting there the largest of precious accomplishments in artistic skill in order to perpetuate their own memories, as well as to enrich their descendants. Our princes were perhaps as rich as they, and possibly as powerful, but their ambitions did not usually extend to a line of posterity. Their palaces were contracted to a "three score and ten" size; for each of them, no matter how wide his capability of enjoyment, knew that it was personal and ended when his little spark of life should be extinguished.

I gladly record, however, that in [137] these later days some of them have made the American world their heirs, and are building and enriching museums and colleges, making them palaces of growth and enlightenment, and so giving to the many what an older race of princes built and enriched and guarded for the few.

But in the meantime what were we to do about our tapestries? They were costly, very costly to produce, and although we took account of the delight of their creation and put it on the credit side of our books, along with the fact that the weekly pay roll of the tapestry room went for the comfort and maintenance of the students whom we loved and cherished, I soon realized the fact that a commercial firm could not be burdened with the fads of any one member. Before I had carried this conclusion to its logical end, we had opportunities of using our skill worthily in several of the new great houses of the time. When the Cornelius Vanderbilt house was erected on Fifth Avenue and Fifty-Seventh Street we received an order for a set of tapestries for the drawing-room walls. These were executed from ideal subjects and of single figures. I remember the "Winged Moon" among them, which was an ideal figure [138] of the new moon lying in a cradle of her own wings. This was but one of the set, one or two of which we afterward made in replica for an exhibit in London. There was no lack of subjects in our background of American history. The legends and beliefs of our North American Indians were full of them, and one of the first we selected was the lovely story of "Minnehaha, Laughing Water," from Longfellow's "Hiawatha." The sketch had been sent to us by Miss Dora Wheeler, as the prize composition of the Saturday Composition Class at Julien's Studio in Paris.

The literary past of the country furnished subjects enough and to spare, and if we wished to walk into the shadowy realms of legend and fiction, there were the picturesque legends of the American Indian from which to choose. Our subjects were often one-figure designs, as such pieces were suitable in size to wall spaces and door openings. Of course commercial considerations could not be lost sight of in our enthusiasm for progress in textile art. Potter Palmer, the multimillionaire of Chicago, was building at the time a palace home on the Lake Shore, and one auspicious day Mrs. Palmer bestowed her beautiful [139] presence upon us, and was mightily

148

taken with our tapestries. Her clever mind was attracted by the "bookishness" of some of the panels of incidents from American literature, and several of them went to beautify the great house on the Lake Shore, in the form of several panels of portraits. Mrs. Palmer was a delightful patron, her own enjoyment of art, in any of its forms, amounted to enthusiasm, and her great physical beauty, to a beauty lover, made every visit from her an epoch. I have never seen the face of an adult woman who has had the experience of wifehood and motherhood which retained so perfectly the flawless beauty of childhood. I have often gazed at the angelic face of some child, and wondered why each year of life should wipe out some exquisite line of drawing, or absorb the entrancing shadows which rest upon the face of childhood. It was a great satisfaction to personally assist in the furnishing of the home of this beautiful aristocrat, whose own law allowed of no infringement by our mighty three, having been shaped in a mind enriched by much classical study and constant acquaintance with the beautiful.

When our embroideries and needlework had [140] taken their place in this country, we were asked to make part of an Exhibition of American Art in London. This we were very glad to do, for the artistic gratification of being able to measure what we were doing with the best art of the kind abroad. It was also pleasant to be considered worthy company with the best in our own land, to rub shoulders with our best painters, our great makers of stained glass, leaders who take genuine pleasure in ideal work. Of course this applies to amateur work only, as professional decoration must accord with the general plan which has been selected.

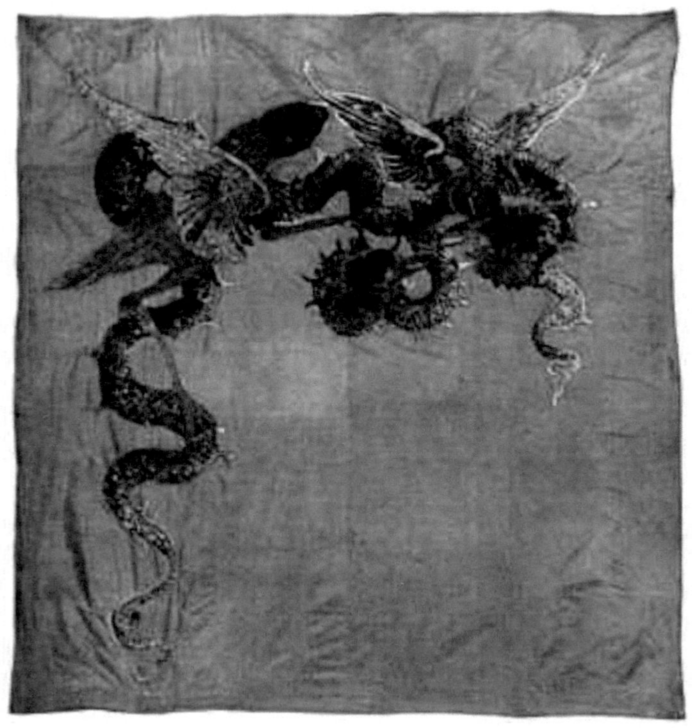

larger image

FIGHTING DRAGONS

Drawn by Candace Wheeler and embroidered by The Associated Artists, 1885.

I had reason to think that the Exhibition made by the Associated Artists at Chicago was of lasting use to all lovers of needlework, the world over, since so many other races came there to get their world lessons. I learned much that was of value to me from familiar study of the exhibits from different countries, from their excellencies and differences and the reasons why such wide divergences existed, and from observation of the people themselves who produced them — for many of the exhibits were in charge of practical needleworkers who knew the history of their art from [141] its very beginning. I found more of interest in Oriental art from seeing that it was not merely a perfunctory repetition of stitches and patterns, but that there was a stanch, almost a religious, integrity in doing the thing exactly as it had been done by generations of forefathers, and that the silks and tissues and flosses and threads of gold were the best the world produced. In the presence of such fidelity, what mattered it that the borders and blocks were formed of angles, or zigzags, or squares, or any other fixed and mechanical shapes? The spirit of it was true to its race and traditions. In the face of it, all our beautiful copies of flowers, and growths, and gracious forms of nature seemed almost experimental—the art of growing and changing nations.

But as we do not make the early art of long existent races models upon which to shape our search for the most beautiful, the persistence of Eastern form in embroidery need not prevent our progress in design. I made an interesting note of this persistence of Eastern design, when, many years ago, I had an opportunity of examining some mummy wrappings from a burial ground at [142] Lima, Peru. They were wonderful weavings of aboriginal cloth, bordered with embroidery done in dyed or colored threads of flax, in designs as purely Eastern as can be found in any ancient or modern Eastern embroidery. How could it happen that the ornamental designs of the Far East and the Far West should touch each other? Was it similarity of thought knowledge, the kinship of the human mind, or some long-forgotten means of transmission of the material and actual, of which we all-knowing moderns do not even dream? This wonderful South American embroidery of past ages antedated many antique remains of the art of stitchery which we treasure with as wide a margin of time as lies between their day and ours.

Embroidery has become a dependence and a business for thousands of women, and it is this which secures its permanence. We may trust skillful executants who live by its practice to keep ahead of the changing fancies of society and invent for it new wants and new fashions. And this, because their chance of living depends upon it, and it promises to be a permanent and growing art. It may, and will, undoubtedly, take [143] on new directions, but it is no longer a lost art. On the contrary, it is one where practice has attained such perfection that it is fully equal to any new demands and quite competent to answer any of the higher calls of art.

CHAPTER VIII   THE BAYEUX TAPESTRIES
[144]

While a description of this most important work of women's hands may seem somewhat irrelevant in a book devoted to the development of the art of embroidery in America, it is so important a link in the subject of stitchery, executed as it was in the eleventh century, that a short chapter on this most interesting and vital subject may not come amiss.

Among all our present possessions of early skill, perhaps nothing is more widely known than what is called the Bayeux Tapestry. This much venerated work is not tapestry at all, but a pictorial record in outline, done with a needle, as simply as though written in ink, at least according to our present understanding of what is known as tapestry.

We read of the subject, and the name of William the Conqueror looms large in the imagination. We think of the tapestry as a great illustrated page of history, large in proportion not alone to the deeds it chronicles, but to their [145] importance in the story of one of the greatest, perhaps, of the modern races; and across this illustrated page we fancy the prancing of war horses and the prowess of the knight, the passing of seas and the march of armies, with all the attendant tragedy of circumstance.

But this is only in one's mind. The reality is a more or less tattered strip of grayish-white linen, two feet in width and two hundred and thirty feet long, and along this frail bridge between the past and present march the actors in the great conquest. It seems but an inadequate pathway, but it has borne its phalanxes of men, its two hundred horses, its five hundred and fifty-five dogs and other animals, its forty-one ships, its numberless castles and trees, its roads and farms safely through all the intervening years from 1066 to 1919, and it still holds them.

In truth, we wonder much over this production of the past, and not alone over the heroes who career so mildly in their armor of colored crewels on the linen background. We wonder, in the first place, how a continuous web of over two hundred feet in length could have been woven. Then, we know that lengths of woven stuffs are [146] limited only by the requirements of commerce, and that Matilda was of Flanders, and her father had learned the princely trick of loving and encouraging manufactures, and had, indeed, taught it to his daughter, and that Flanders was a noted center of manufacture. Then we decide that if Matilda had called for a strip of linen two thousand feet long, whereon to write the warlike history of a spouse who began his gentle part toward her (for so history avers) by pulling her from her horse and rolling her in the mud because she refused to marry him, it would have been forthcoming as easily as two hundred. Should the Queen of England require a stretch of linen as long as from England to America, whereon to record the successes of her reign, who doubts that it would be supplied her?

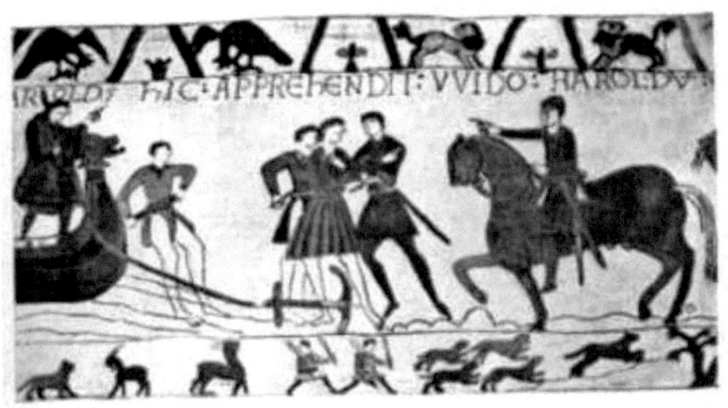
HIC : APPREHENDIT : VVIDO : HAROLDVM

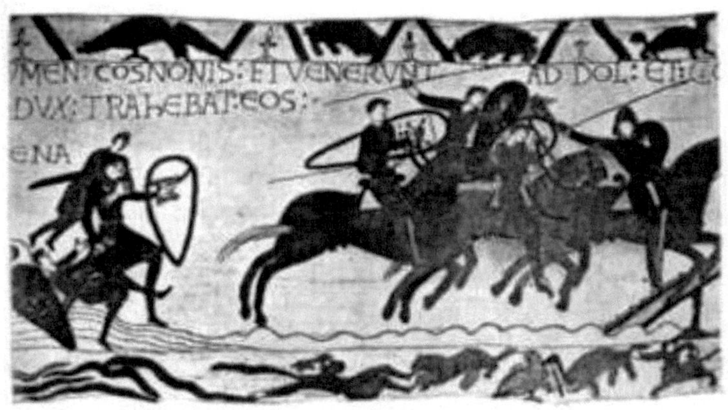
MEN : COSNONIS : ET VENERVNT AD DOL : ET CO
DVX : TRAHEBAT : EOS
ENA

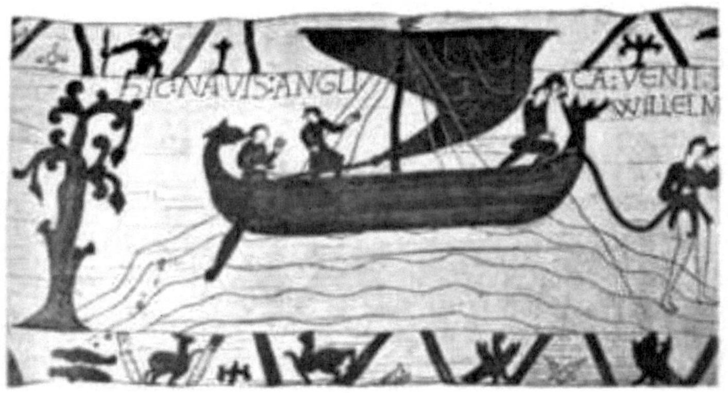
HIC NAVIS ANGLI CA : VENIT
WILLELM

larger image

THREE SCENES FROM THE BAYEUX TAPESTRY

So, when the question of this web is disposed of, we wonder who drew all these figures of men and horses, for Queen Matilda and her ladies to overlay with stitchery, and why his name has not come down to us. We decide within our minds, for it never occurs to us to impute such ability in drawing to the Queen or her ladies, that it was the work of some monkish brother who [147] varied his illuminating labor upon missals and copies of the Scripture by doing these worldly and interesting things.

We think of the never to be forgotten Gerard in *The Cloister and the Hearth*, and wonder if it was some monastery-trained youth like him who rested from the creation of saints and angels upon vellum, to draw fighting knights upon linen, and whether, perchance, his hushed heart burned within him at the stir and valor of the deeds he portrayed. And then some one, better informed than we, points out the figure of a dwarf, nicely labeled as Turold—for many of the actors in this embroidered story are labeled in delicate stitches—and tells us that his was the hand that set the copy for all the happy and beloved maids of the Queen, and the hapless and perhaps equally beloved Saxon maids. We wonder, again, how these skillful and noble Saxons like to find themselves thus writing their own infelicities and humiliations for all the world to see, and then—for so does the human mind go groping into motives and springs of action—we wonder if their famous skill in needlework, of which the wide-awake Matilda must surely have known, put it [148] into her head to make this curious life-record of her great lord, and we reflect that if it were so, it would only be another facet of her many-sided ability.

But that was underneath the surface. Outside was the queenly magnificence and wifely glorification of her lot, a smooth current of irresistible prosperity. Underneath was the whirling and buzzing of the wheels of thought, the springs of motion which governed the great current.

In truth, two such clever thought centers as William of Normandy and Matilda of Flanders seldom in the world have made a conjunction, or we would have had more great conquests to record. We may fancy what we will in the far background which this slender length of linen reaches, all the byplay which accompanied the guarded life of the castle, the religious life of the cathedral and monastery, the colored and bannered pomp of duke and noble.

It was all mightily picturesque, with its contrasts of gorgeousness and privation, but probably Matilda the dexterous thought that times were good enough when she could sit in safety, surrounded by her maids and priests, and write her [149] royal journal as she pleased, with a threaded stylus; and well for us that she elected to do this, although her records are written in so quaint a fashion that amusement and interest are twin spectators of the result.

Two borders, upper and lower, remind one irresistibly of a child's processional picture on a slate. The figures are done in outline only, colors corresponding to those used in the body of the work. Each border is some six inches wide, and has the air of a little running commentary or enlargement of the main story. There are variations and incidents which could not perhaps be put down in the main body, where all the figures are worked solidly in the stitch which has been rechristened "Kensington stitch." The horses are worked in red-brown and gray crewels, some of them duly spotted and dappled, the banners and gonfalons carefully wrought in the colors and devices belonging to them. The whole work follows scrupulously the scenes of the Conquest, giving the lives of the actors both in Normandy and England, as well as the transit from one country to the other.

The first scene evidently represents Edward the [150] Confessor giving audience to Harold, the last of the Saxon kings. The next gives the embarkation of Harold, and the third his capture in France.

Then comes the death of Edward, and the tapestry story struggles ineffectually with the incidents of his death and funeral; and the election of Harold as King of England, showing him seated crowned and in royal robes under a very primitive canopy. After this, the scene shifts again to France, and portrays the preparations for invasion made by the Duke of Normandy, who was called by the people of the country he invaded "William the Conqueror," and who have continued to know him only by that name through all succeeding centuries, the shame and sorrow of vanquishment quite buried under the glory of the performance, Saxon and Norman uniting in esteem of the successful result.

All this history is duly set forth in archaic simplicity by the stitches of Queen Matilda, who, in preserving the record of the deeds of her doughty lord, has set down also a record of herself as the ideal wife, who glorifies her husband, and merges all she is of woman into that condition—and still it is only a strip of linen worked in [151] crewels. All the triumphs of the great Conqueror are written upon it, but none of the disappointments. The needlework story does not relate (how could it when Matilda's active, trained and industrious fingers had been stilled by death?) the sorrows which overcame even her fortunate hero—that his body was robbed of its clothing, and lay naked and dishonored beside a disputed grave, where even the solemn claim of death to burial was resisted until an old wrong "done in the body" was righted. And though his son reigned after him, and he founded a royal line, perhaps one of the greatest enjoyments of his successful life consisted in watching the fingers of his well-beloved Matilda as they worked this linen record.

Of course it is the great events it portrays and the human interest it holds which make this tapestry exceedingly valuable, for, artistically, it is of no more value than a child's sampler. But, simple as it is, volumes have been written about it. Scholars and historians have pored over its pictured history, money without stint has been spent in paper reproductions of it, and, finally, the whole important embroidery society [152] of Leeds, England, spent two industrious years in copying it, and earned fame and envy thereby.

The wonderful remains of the work of skilled fingers serve to dignify the art of which it is capable, and to sing a varied song in the ears of the modern embroiderer, who follows her own will in spite of time-hallowed examples. The women of today, 1920, have been called to work that is widely different from that of the ages when embroidery was a natural recourse and almost universal practice, but it is an art which has done too much for the progress of the world, in all its different phases, to die, or to cease to progress. There will always be quiet souls, whose lives have been made so by circumstances, who will find solace in the practice of needlework,

so we may safely leave with them an art which has done so much
for mankind.

THE END